Contents

What Is Force?

What makes a rocket launch into the sky or a sled speed down a hill? **Forces** make things move. A force is a push or a pull. Forces are everywhere. You cannot see a force, but you can see what it does. A pull opens a door. A push makes a toy car speed away.

Forces cause objects to move, but not always. What would happen if you and your friend each pulled on opposite ends of a rope? If you both tugged with **equal** force, the rope would stay in place. If you used greater force than your friend, the rope would move toward you. When the forces on an object at rest are **balanced** (equal), the object stays at rest. When the forces are **unbalanced** (not equal), the object moves.

Define It!

balanced: equal forces acting on an object

equal: the same

force: a push or a pull

unbalanced: unequal forces acting on an object

Concepts:

Forces make things move.

Forces can be balanced or unbalanced.

Forces and Motion

Look at each picture. Write *push* or *pull* to describe the force being used.

Philip Bird / Shutterstock.com

_____

_____

_____

Forces and Motion

Friction

Friction is a force between objects that are touching. When **surfaces** rub together, they grab on to each other. Friction slows down a moving object.

Think of a box sitting on a table. The box is not moving because the forces on it are balanced. If you push it, the forces become unbalanced and the box slides across the table. Will the box slide forever? No, because friction between the box and the table will slow the box down until it stops. Most often, a smooth surface has less friction than a rough surface.

Sometimes friction can be helpful. Friction makes the tires and brakes stop a bike. Boots with rough soles have more friction to keep you from slipping on an icy sidewalk.

Define It!

friction: a force that slows down the motion of an object that is touching something else as it moves

surface: the outer layer

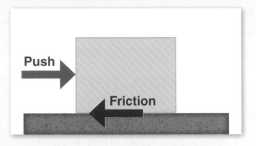

Circle the answer.

1. Which one would work best with greater friction?

tires and brakes

slide

2. Which one would work best with little friction?

snow boots

sled

Force and Motion

Forces change the **motion** of objects. Forces make objects speed up and slow down. Forces make objects change direction and change shape.

Define It!

direction: the line along which something travels

motion: the act of moving

size: the amount of something

Jordan Tan / Shutterstock.com

speed up   **slow down**   **change direction**   **change shape**

A force has both **size** and **direction**. Think about a soccer ball. What happens when you try to make a goal? To get the ball into the goal, you kick it with the right amount (size) of force. If you use too little force, the ball will not reach the goal. You also aim (direct) the force so that the ball goes into the net. If the direction of the force is off, the ball will miss the goal.

Draw a line under the answer.

1. Squeezing a tube of toothpaste shows that force can _____.

   slow things down   **change the shape of things**

2. Batting a baseball shows that force changes the _____ of an object.

   direction   **size**

Forces and Motion

Forces and Motion

Picturing Forces

Forces cannot be seen, but we can see what they do. Forces change the motion of objects. In order to show how forces work, scientists make drawings. Arrows in the drawings show the direction of the forces. Arrows also show the size of the forces. A longer arrow stands for a stronger force.

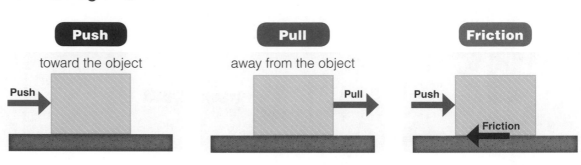

Push
toward the object

Pull
away from the object

Friction

Look at the force drawing chart. Make a check mark to show if the forces are balanced or unbalanced.

	Force Drawing	Balanced Forces	Unbalanced Forces
1			
2			
3			
4			

Explain your answer for number 2.

_____

_____

_____

Either/Or Questions

Write each answer.

1. Is a push a size **or** a force? _____

2. Is a pull a force **or** a surface? _____

3. If forces are balanced, are they equal **or** unequal? _____

4. Does friction slow things down **or** speed things up? _____

5. If an object moves, is it at rest **or** in motion? _____

6. Is the surface of a slide smooth **or** rough? _____

7. Does the direction of a force control how far an object goes **or** where an object goes? _____

8. Are unbalanced forces equal **or** unequal? _____

9. Does the size of a force change the speed of an object **or** the direction of an object? _____

10. Is a force seen **or** unseen? _____

Think About It

Is a force real or unreal? How do you know?

_____

_____

Forces and Motion

Physical Science: Forces

Marshmallow Popper

How far can you make a marshmallow fly? This activity shows how the size of a force changes the distance an object travels.

Skill:
Conduct a simple scientific investigation to answer the question "how?"

Forces and Motion

What You Need

- yogurt cup
- scissors
- balloon
- mini marshmallows
- sidewalk chalk

What You Do

1. Ask an adult to cut out the bottom of a yogurt cup.

2. Tie a knot at the open end of the balloon and cut off about ½" (1.3 cm) from the other end.

3. Stretch the cut end of the balloon over the top rim of the yogurt cup.

4. Go outside on a paved surface if possible. Drop a mini marshmallow into the cup, pull back on the knotted end of the balloon, aim into the distance, and let go.

5. How far did the marshmallow travel? Mark the place where it landed with sidewalk chalk. How can you make the distance longer or shorter? Test your idea. Mark each landing place.

6. Pulling back on the balloon and then letting go creates a force that pushes the marshmallow.

How did you make the force greater?

_____

How did the size of a force change the distance traveled by the marshmallow?

_____

_____

Friction in Action

What You Need

- toy car
- 3 cardboard pieces about 4" x 18" (10 x 46 cm)
- 3 coverings such as crinkled or smooth foil, bubble wrap, sandpaper, wax paper, paper towel, or other materials
- tape
- 3 stacks of books or a long rectangular object
- measuring tape

What You Do

1. Make three toy car ramps from cardboard. Make them all the same length, about 18" (46 cm) long.

2. Cover each ramp with a different covering and tape it. Use both smooth and rough coverings to create different amounts of friction.

3. Prop one end of each ramp on a stack of books or a long rectangular object as shown. If you are using stacks of books, make sure that they are all the same height.

4. Start the car at the top and let it go down the ramp without pushing it. For each ramp, measure the distance the car travels from the bottom edge of the ramp. Write it down.

I found out that the ramp covered with _____ had the least friction.

Skills:

Predict the outcome of a simple investigation and compare the result with the prediction.

Forces and Motion

Show What You Know

Look at the picture. List two examples of each force at work.

Pull

1. _____

2. _____

Push

1. _____

2. _____

Forces are everywhere, and we use them every day. Think back to this morning and the things you did after you got up. Describe what you did and tell if you used a *push* or a *pull*.

_____

_____

_____

_____

_____

Forces and Motion

Magnets Attract Metals

Concept:

Magnets are attracted to metals with iron.

What makes the notes stick on this refrigerator door? Not glue, but an unseen force called **magnetism**!

Magnetism is the force that makes **magnets** pull, or **attract**, some kinds of metal. The metal refrigerator door is attracted to magnets. A magnet will not attract glass, plastic, wood, or anything else that does not contain metal.

Magnets stick to objects made of metal, but not all metals. The metal **iron**, or a metal that has iron in it, is attracted to a magnet. A magnet won't stick to coins or soda cans. They are not made of iron.

1. Draw an **X** on the objects that will **not** be attracted to a magnet.

2. Which objects above may have iron in them? How could you test them?

_____

_____

_____

Magnets

Physical Science: Forces

Magnets Push and Pull

Define It!

magnetic field: the space around a magnet where its force can be found

pole: either end of a magnet

repel: to push away

All magnets have a **magnetic field** that you cannot see. It's the area around the magnet where a force pulls objects toward the magnet. Magnets have two **poles**. The poles are the parts of the magnet where its force is the strongest. Every magnet has a north pole and a south pole. **N** stands for *north* and **S** stands for *south*.

When two magnets are held with their north and south poles together, the poles attract each other. They pull together. But two poles of the same kind **repel** one another. They push away.

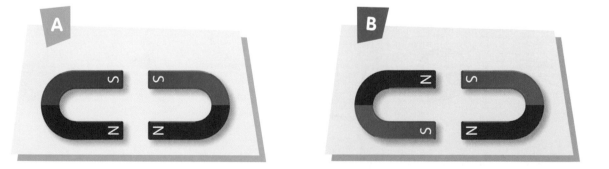

1. Which picture shows magnets that will attract?   **A   B**

2. Which picture shows magnets that will repel?   **A   B**

Magnets: Strong or Weak?

Define It!

magnetic: able to attract iron or act like a magnet

strength: power

weak: lacking strength

Concept:
Magnets have a magnetic field.

Which magnets are stronger—big ones or small ones? You cannot know the strength of a magnet just by its size. The **strength** of a magnet has to do with its magnetic field. A strong **magnetic** field will attract more than a **weak** magnetic field will. The stronger magnetic field will attract things that are farther away or that are heavier.

Look at these two magnets. You cannot see the magnetic force around a magnet. But the lines in these pictures show where the magnetic fields are. The field shown with more lines is stronger. Trace the magnetic fields.

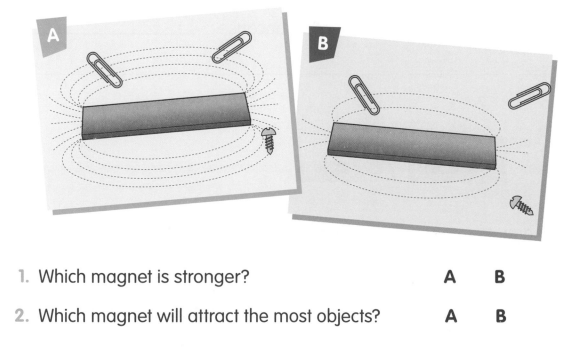

1. Which magnet is stronger?   A   B

2. Which magnet will attract the most objects?   A   B

Looking at Magnets

Magnets **attract** when the north and south poles are put together. Magnets **repel** when two poles that are alike are put together.

Trace the arrows that show the magnetic forces in each picture. Complete the sentence to tell what is happening in each picture and why. Use the words *attract* and *repel*.

1

The magnets _____ each other because _____

_____

2

The magnets _____ each other because _____

_____

3

The magnets _____ each other because _____

_____

Review the Words

Read each clue and write the missing word on the lines.

| repel | wood | field | iron | poles |

1. The space around a magnet that attracts metal is its

____ ____ ____ ____ ____.

2. A magnet attracts metal with ____ ____ ____ ____ in it.

3. Another word that means "to push away" is ____ ____ ____ ____ ____.

4. A magnet has two ____ ____ ____ ____ ____: north and south.

5. Magnets do not attract objects made of ____ ____ ____ ____.

Write the letters from the yellow boxes to answer the riddle.

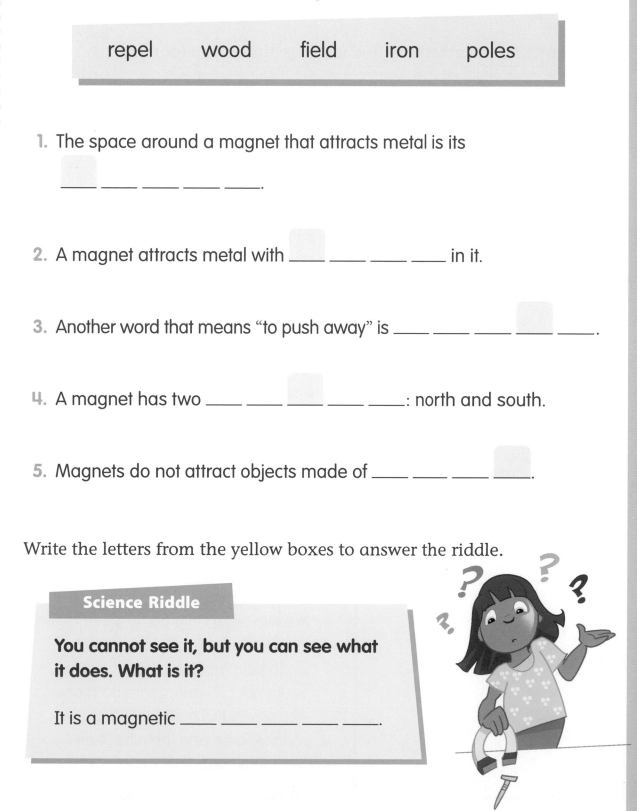

Science Riddle

You cannot see it, but you can see what it does. What is it?

It is a magnetic ____ ____ ____ ____ ____.

Magnets

Skills:
Conduct a
simple scientific
investigation and
record results.

Magnet Scavenger Hunt

Go on a hunt around your house. First, find a magnet. Then look for items that will stick to the magnet. Which things will **not** stick?

Complete this chart. Draw and label six things you found.

Magnetic	Not Magnetic

What shape is your magnet?
Draw it here.

Did You Know?

Magnets come in different sizes and shapes, but they all have a north and a south pole. On a bar magnet or a horseshoe magnet, one end is the north pole and the other end is the south pole. If your magnet is a disc, one side is the north pole. Flip the magnet over, and the other side is the south pole.

Magnets

Make Bottle Cap Magnets

What You Need

- bottle caps
- patterned paper
- clear packing tape
- gems, beads, buttons
- self-adhesive disc magnets (available in craft stores)
- scissors
- glue

Glue

What You Do

1. Cut a circle from patterned paper to fit inside the bottle cap.

2. Protect the paper circle by placing it between two pieces of clear packing tape. Then trim the circle and glue it to the inside of the bottle cap.

3. You may wish to glue gems, beads, or buttons inside the bottle cap to decorate it.

4. Peel and stick a magnet to the back.

5. Go around the house and discover where your magnetic bottle cap will stick!

Note: Do **not** stick your magnet on a computer, monitor, watch, or hearing aid.

Magnets

Apply What You Learned

Test the strength of two magnets to find out which magnet is stronger. Use two magnets and a handful of paper clips. Write about your investigation and draw sketches to show what you did.

Skills:
Conduct a simple scientific investigation and record results.

Hint

To test the strength of two magnets, find out how much each magnet can pick up at one time.

1. **Define the Problem:** What do you want to find out?

_____

2. **Design a Test:** What will you do? _____

_____

_____

3. **Record Your Data:** Write what you saw when you did the test.

_____

_____

_____

_____

Draw what you saw.

4. **Write About the Results:** What did you find out?

_____

Skill Sharpeners—Science • EMC 5323 • © Evan-Moor Corp.

About Gravity

Define It!

gravity: a force that pulls objects together

Isaac Newton: a famous English scientist and mathematician (1642–1727)

law: in science, an observed fact that something always happens under the same conditions

scientist: someone who is an expert in a science

Concepts:

Gravity is a force that holds us on Earth.

Isaac Newton had the idea that there must be a force pulling things to Earth's center.

Gravity is a force that pulls objects toward each other. Although you cannot see it, the force of gravity is everywhere. Earth's gravity pulls in one direction—down. A better way of saying that is, gravity pulls you and everything on Earth toward Earth's center. Gravity is what holds us on Earth.

Isaac Newton was a **scientist** who lived more than 300 years ago. Newton was the first to figure out that there must be a force pulling things to Earth's center. A famous story says that Newton saw an apple fall from a tree. This made him wonder why things fall down and not sideways or up. He thought there must be a force in Earth's center that pulls everything toward it. No one knows for sure if the story about the apple is true, but Newton's **law** of gravity was very important to science.

Complete the sentences.

1. An apple falls down from a tree, instead of up, because

   _____.

2. _____ thought about why objects fall to Earth.

Everything Has Gravity

Gravity is a force that **attracts**. Everything has gravity, which means everything pulls on everything else. Some objects have a stronger pull than others. Even your body has gravity, but its pull on the things around you is very weak.

The size of the force of gravity depends on the **mass** of an object. An object's mass is how much **matter**, or "stuff," it has. For example, Earth has much more mass than a basketball does, so Earth has a much greater pull. Because of the strong pull of Earth's gravity, the basketball will always fall to Earth no matter how hard it is thrown. And because Earth has much more mass than you do, you will not float off Earth into space.

Circle the answer.

1. Which one has more gravity?

girl   **Earth**

2. Which one has more mass?

book   **Earth**

Gravity

Gravity and Weight

Define It!

astronaut: a person who travels to outer space

weight: a measure of the pull of gravity on an object

weightless: having no gravity pulling on it

To a scientist, mass and **weight** are not the same thing. Your weight is a measure of the pull of gravity on you. **Astronauts** traveling in space are **weightless** because there is no gravity pulling on them. Their weight is zero. But their mass is the same as it was on Earth.

Other planets, moons, and stars have their own gravity. So if you visited other worlds, your weight would be different from your weight on Earth. A person who weighs 60 pounds (about 27 kg) on Earth would only weigh about 23 pounds (about 10 kg) on Mars. The same person would weigh about 142 pounds (about 64 kg) on Jupiter.

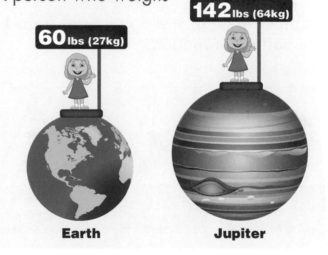

60 lbs (27kg)

142 lbs (64kg)

Earth   Jupiter

Gravity

Earth has a very large mass. This means that it has a strong force of gravity, too. The moon is smaller than Earth and has less gravity. Would you weigh more on the moon or less? Why?

_____

_____

_____

Playground Forces

Have you ever looked at a playground to see forces in action? Let's look at what happens when Ava sits on a swing. A force is needed to set the swing in motion. The swing will move when someone pushes Ava or when she pulls back and pumps her legs. After that, forces carry Ava up and gravity pulls her down. You can predict the pattern of motion. If the swing goes forward and up, next it will go down. Then the swing will go backward and up, and down again. When Ava drags her feet on the ground, she creates enough force to stop the swing. If Ava simply stopped pumping her legs, the swing would stop by itself because of the force of the air.

Number these mixed-up pictures from **1** to **5** to show the pattern of motion.

_____   _____   1   _____   3

Why does the swing always come down again?

_____

_____

Physical Science: Forces   Skill Sharpeners—Science • EMC 5323 • © Evan-Moor Corp.

Gravity Crossword Puzzle

Use the vocabulary words to complete the crossword puzzle.

attract	weight	gravity	Newton
matter	weightless	scientist	astronaut

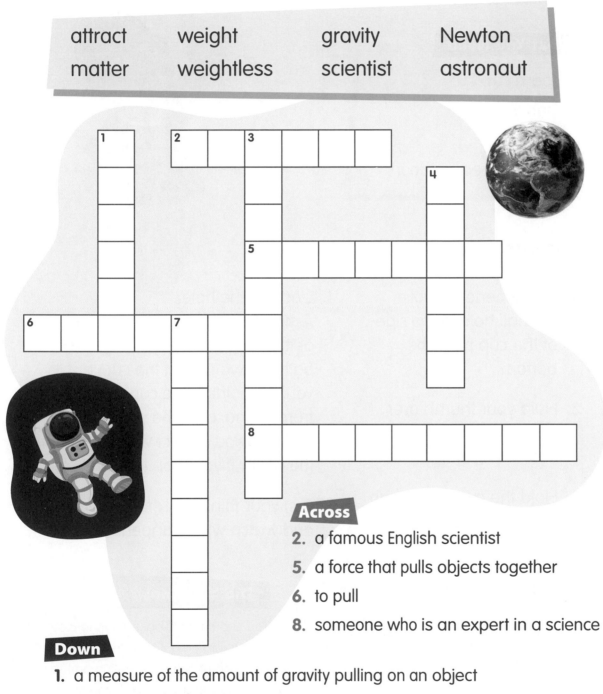

Across

2. a famous English scientist
5. a force that pulls objects together
6. to pull
8. someone who is an expert in a science

Down

1. a measure of the amount of gravity pulling on an object
3. having no gravity pulling on it
4. something that takes up space and has weight
7. a person who travels to outer space

Physical Science: Forces

Falling Water

Experiment with water to find out more about the effects of gravity on falling objects.

What You Need

- foam cup
- pencil
- water
- grassy area outdoors

What You Do

1. Use a pencil to poke a small hole in the side of the cup near the bottom.

2. Hold your thumb over the hole as you fill the cup with water.

3. Hold the cup up as high as you can reach.

4. Uncover the hole. A stream of water will squirt out of the cup! Gravity is pulling on both the water and the cup, but you are holding the cup to keep it from falling. Only the water can fall. What do you predict will happen to the water if you drop the cup?

5. Test your thinking. Let the cup drop and watch what happens.

What did you observe the water do?

_____

_____

_____

_____

Did You Know?

You should have observed the water stop squirting out as the cup fell. That's because gravity was pulling on the cup and the water equally. Even though their masses are different, both the cup and the water were falling at the same rate of speed.

Gravity

Paper Roller Coaster

If you have ever ridden a roller coaster, you know the pull of gravity can be fun! Making a roller coaster sculpture is fun, too.

What You Need

- 12" x 18" (30 x 46 cm) sheet of poster board
- glue and tape
- scissors
- colored construction paper
- ruler
- crayons or markers
- small piece of tissue paper or other thin paper

What You Do

1. Measure and cut construction paper into long strips 1½" to 2" (4 to 5 cm) wide for the coaster tracks. Decorate the tracks with different patterns.

2. Roll a 6" x 6" (15 x 15 cm) square of construction paper into a tube to use to hold up the tracks. Tape it. Cut ½" (1.3 cm) slits in the bottom of the tube to make tabs for gluing.

3. Let the poster board be your base. Glue the paper tube in one corner of the base. Tape one end of a track to the top of the tube and glue the other end to the poster board.

4. To form the rest of the roller coaster, glue one end of a strip to the poster board. Twist the paper strip and then glue the other end to the poster board. Continue connecting the paper strips in this way.

5. Crumple a paper ball from the thin paper. Send it rolling down different parts of your roller coaster to show the force of gravity.

Gravity

Skills:

Explain the relationship between the motion of an object and the pull of gravity.

Illustrate the forces acting on objects.

Gravity on the Playground

Go to a playground to look for gravity in action. Describe in which direction gravity pulls you. Draw a picture showing the slide, swings, monkey bars, seesaw, or other objects. Then add force arrows to show the pull of gravity.

_____

_____

_____

_____

_____

_____

Draw

From Seed to Plant

Concepts:

Reproduction is essential to the continued existence of every kind of organism.

Plants undergo a series of orderly changes in their life cycles.

Organisms have structures and functions that help them survive in an environment.

Define It!

conditions: the weather, soil, and light affecting growth

develop: to grow into an adult

germinate: to begin to grow; to sprout

root: a plant part that grows down into the soil

A seed doesn't look like the plant it will become. But inside are the tiny beginnings of a **root** and a stem. The seed has a food supply, too. A seed coat covers and protects everything inside the seed.

When **conditions** are right, the seed will **germinate**, or grow. Warmth from the sun, water from the rain, and food from the soil make the right conditions for growth.

As a plant grows taller, it also **develops** new parts. Its new leaves help make food for the plant. New roots hold it in the soil. Many plants develop flowers.

Write the answer to each question.

1. What protects a seed? _____

2. What happens to a seed when conditions are right? _____

3. What new plant parts develop? _____

Life Cycles

Flowers and Their Seeds

Almost all plants on Earth have flowers. Flowers are beautiful to look at and they smell good, but they also do important work for the plant. Flowers make seeds, which are needed for the plant to **reproduce**, or make new plants. Sometimes the seeds drop to the ground. Other seeds are carried away and dropped by animals or by the wind. Many flowering plants produce their seeds and then die. When the conditions are right, the seeds will produce new plants. A whole new **life cycle** will begin.

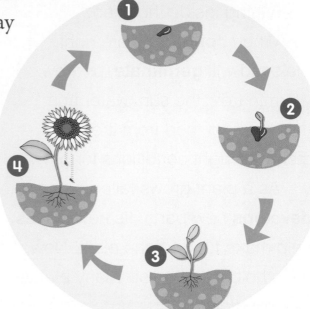

Write the missing words.

1. Seeds help a plant to make new plants, or _____.

2. A plant germinates, grows and develops, reproduces, and dies. This is called its _____.

3. Seeds can be carried by _____ or _____.

Insects Carry Pollen

Flowers make seeds when **pollen** travels from the **stamen** of a flower to the **pistil**. Insects such as bees, moths, and butterflies help carry pollen from one flower to another. When an insect lands on a flower, pollen sticks to the insect. When the insect visits another flower, some of the pollen falls off its body and **pollinates** that flower.

Define It!

pistil: the part of a flower in which seeds develop

pollen: tiny grains that help a plant produce seeds

pollinates: brings pollen to a plant

stamen: the part of a flower with pollen at the tip

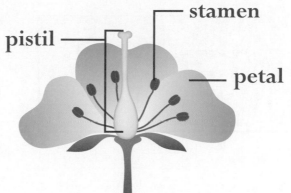

pistil

stamen

petal

Concepts:

Plants undergo a series of orderly changes in their life cycles.

Organisms have structures and functions that help them survive in an environment.

Number the events below in the correct order.

_____ The bee lands on a flower to eat and drink.

_____ The bee flies to another flower.

_____ Pollen sticks to the bee.

_____ The flower makes seeds.

_____ Pollen falls off the bee.

Write the words to complete the sentence.

When a bee carries _____ from one flower

to another, the bee _____ the flower.

Life Cycles

Burrs and Fur

Some plants make seeds that have little hooks. These hooks can attach to animals passing by. Barley is a type of grass plant that moves its seeds in this way.

Look at each picture below. Then write the letter of the sentence that matches that picture.

How Barley Distributes Its Seeds

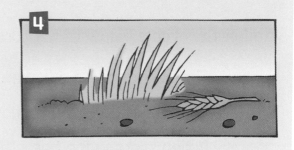

_____

_____

_____

_____

a. The dog scratches and sheds the seeds.

b. The dog rubs against the grass.

c. Seeds land on the ground and later grow into new plants.

d. Barley seeds attach themselves to the dog's fur.

Life Cycles

Review the Words

Skill:

Apply content vocabulary in context sentences.

Read each clue and write the missing word on the lines.

germinate pollen reproduce stamen

1. The pistil and the ___ ___ ___ ___ ___ ___ are parts of a flower.

2. When conditions are right, a tiny seed will ___ ___ ___ ___ ___ ___ ___ ___ ___.

3. Tiny grains of ___ ___ ___ ___ ___ ___ stick to an insect.

4. Flowers ___ ___ ___ ___ ___ ___ ___ ___ ___ by making seeds.

Write the letters from the yellow boxes to answer the riddle.

Science Riddle

Where does a tiny plant hide?

inside every ___ ___ ___ ___

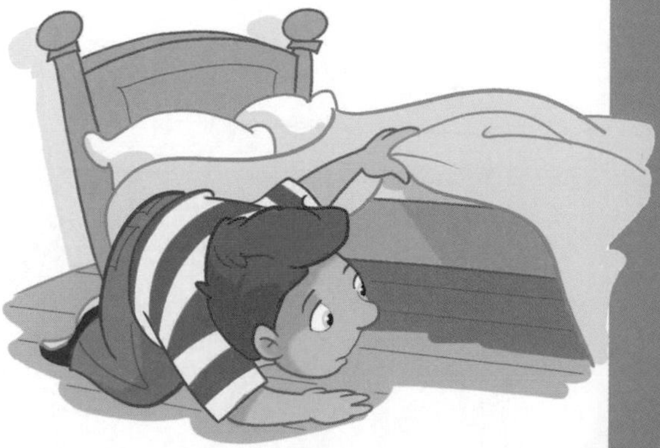

Bean Sprout in a Bag

When you plant a seed in soil, you cannot see it germinate. But here is an easy way to watch a bean seed germinate. Prepare to be amazed!

What You Need

- dried beans
- paper towels
- plastic sandwich bags with a zipper
- masking tape

What You Do

1. Fold a paper towel to fit in a plastic sandwich bag. Sprinkle the paper towel with enough water to make it damp before you place it in the bag. It should not be dripping wet, just moist.

2. Place a dried bean on the paper towel and zip the bag.

3. Tape the bag in a warm place, such as on a window that gets some sunlight. Hang it so you can observe the bean inside.

4. Put together and hang two more bags just in case the first one doesn't work. The beans should germinate in a few days.

5. Keep a journal of what you observe each day, beginning with today. If the paper towel dries out, add a few drops of water.

6. After about two weeks, plant the sprouts in a pot of soil, with their leaves above the soil. Or, if the weather is warm and sunny, plant them outdoors.

Life Cycles

Plant-Print Papers

Skill:

Follow a sequence of directions to complete a nature project.

What You Need

- leaves and flowers
- heavy drawing paper
- paper towels
- cutting board
- small hammer or rubber mallet
- newspaper

What You Do

1. Collect leaves and flowers from your yard. Not all leaves and flowers will work for this project, so choose different kinds to try.

2. Find a surface that a hammer won't hurt, such as a cutting board. Cover the surface with a pad of newspapers. Place a sheet of drawing paper on top of the newspapers.

3. Arrange some plant parts on the drawing paper in a pretty design. Cover this with three layers of paper towels.

4. Carefully tap the layers with the hammer. (Watch your fingers!) The natural colors of the plants will print on the paper.

5. Peek under the paper towels to see if you want to tap some more. When you are done, peel away the plant parts.

6. Use your beautiful papers to make bookmarks or cards.

Life Cycles

Life Cycle of a Plant

Look at the diagram of the life cycle of a plant. Describe each step of the life cycle on the lines below.

❶ _____

_____

❷ _____

_____

❸ _____

_____

❹ _____

_____

Life Cycles

Food for Growth

Concepts:

Living things need energy to grow and develop.

Animals get energy from food.

Define It!

energy: strength or power

nestling: a baby bird too young to leave the nest

nonliving: not living

organism: a living thing

Living things are different from **nonliving** things. One difference is that a living thing grows and changes, or develops. To do this, a living thing needs **energy**. Animals get their energy from food. Many young animals need help getting food, so their parents feed them. A kitten drinks milk from its mother's body. Robin **nestlings** open their beaks and their parents feed them. You need energy from healthful foods in order to grow and develop, just as other **organisms** do.

Write the answer to each question.

1. What do organisms need in order to grow and develop? _____

2. Where do living things get energy? _____

Growth and Change

Concept:

Different types of animals grow and develop at different rates.

Growth and Change

Fast and Slow Growth

Rabbits are **mammals** that grow and develop quickly. A baby rabbit grows in its mother's body for about a month before it is born. A baby rabbit is called a *kit*. Rabbit kits are born without fur. The kits leave the nest when they are only two weeks old. By six months old, a rabbit is an adult and can start its own family. Rabbits live for about nine years.

Turtles are **reptiles** that grow and develop slowly for years. Some types of turtles grow for 10 years before having **offspring**, and others might grow for 30 years. Turtle eggs hatch in about two to three months. **Hatchlings** are on their own at birth. Their shells are soft at first and do not protect them. The hatchlings must scurry off to hide in a safe place. Some turtles live for 120 years or more.

Fill in the data.

1. Life cycle in years:

    Rabbit _____

    Turtle _____

2. Age when they leave the nest:

    Rabbit _____

    Turtle _____

Big Changes

Some animals make a very big change as they develop. This change is called **metamorphosis**.

Butterfly: Complete Metamorphosis

A butterfly develops in four stages: egg, **larva**, **pupa**, and adult. The egg is laid on a plant. A caterpillar, or larva, hatches from the egg. The caterpillar then becomes a pupa. The pupa sticks to a twig and forms a hard shell called a **chrysalis**. In the spring, an adult butterfly pushes out of the chrysalis.

Dragonfly: Incomplete Metamorphosis

A dragonfly develops in three stages: egg, **nymph**, and adult. Dragonflies lay their eggs in water. When a nymph hatches from an egg, it does not have wings yet. The nymph grows and sheds its skin. This is called **molting**. The nymph molts many times before it grows wings and leaves the water to fly off.

Define It!

chrysalis: a hard shell

larva: a wingless insect form

metamorphosis: a series of changes

molt: to shed an outer covering

nymph: a young insect stage

pupa: an insect stage after larva

A butterfly is coming out of its chrysalis.

A nymph is molting.

Concept:

Some animals change entirely as they develop. This change is called metamorphosis.

Circle *true* or *false*.

1. Both butterflies and dragonflies molt.   true   false

2. Butterflies and dragonflies go through metamorphosis.   true   false

Skill:

Analyze and interpret information presented in a visual format.

What's Inside an Egg?

Chickens and other birds lay eggs in order to reproduce. A chicken egg holds the beginnings of growth.

Read about some of the parts of a chicken egg. Then label each part to complete the diagram.

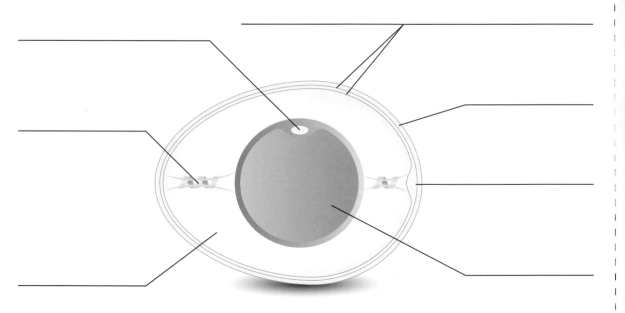

1. **Shell:** Hard outer covering that protects the egg. Water and air can pass through the shell.

2. **Inner and outer membranes:** Thin but strong layers that protect the egg.

3. **Air cell:** Empty space at the larger end of the egg, between membranes.

4. **Chalaza:** (kuh-LAY-zuh) Two ropes of egg white that hold the yolk in place.

5. **Albumen:** Clear liquid, also called the egg white, because it turns white when it is cooked.

6. **Yolk:** Yellow part of the egg. It is food for the developing chick.

7. **Germinal disk:** Small white circle on the yolk, which can develop into a chick.

Life Science: Cycles

Either/Or Questions

Write each answer.

Skill:

Apply content vocabulary.

1. Is an organism living **or** nonliving? _____

2. Is a nestling a kitten **or** a baby bird? _____

3. Does energy come from food **or** a hard shell? _____

4. Is a rabbit a reptile **or** a mammal? _____

5. Are hatchlings a safe place **or** offspring? _____

6. Is metamorphosis a change **or** a chrysalis? _____

7. Is a chrysalis a hard shell **or** an adult insect? _____

8. Does a nymph stick to a twig **or** molt? _____

9. Is a reptile warm-blooded **or** cold-blooded? _____

10. Is a caterpillar a larva **or** a mammal? _____

Growth and change

Skill:

Follow a sequence of directions to complete a chart of scientific data.

I Have Grown

When you were born you probably measured about 20 inches (50 cm) long, as most babies do. How much have you grown since then?

1. Have someone measure your height with a measuring tape.

2. Fill in the data chart about yourself. (If you don't know how long you measured at birth, use 20 inches/50 cm.)

Data About Me!

When I was born, I measured _____ inches/cm long.

Today, I measure _____ inches/cm tall.

I have grown _____ inches/cm taller since I was a newborn.

My eye color is _____.

My hair color is _____.

I write with my _____ hand.

I _____ have freckles. (do/do not)

I _____ wear glasses. (do/do not)

Growth and Change

I Have Grown

What You Need

- a helper
- large sheet of butcher paper
- scissors
- crayons, pencils, markers, paint

What You Do

1. Use a large sheet of butcher paper that is a little taller than you are.

2. Lie on the paper and have someone trace your body outline with a crayon.

3. Cut out the shape, leaving some paper at the bottom for the ground. Draw and color your hair, clothing, shoes, and the ground with crayons.

4. Use a pencil to draw the features of your face. Then go over the pencil lines with paint or markers. Finish coloring in with crayons.

5. Hang your life-sized look-alike on your wall or door.

Growth and change

Hatchlings and Newborns

Read the clues about baby animals. Draw a line from the word to the picture. Then label the picture.

giraffe	human
duckling	sea turtle

Did You Know?

Hatchlings and newborns are able to do different things for themselves. Some need their parents to feed and care for them. Others are on their own right away.

1. These hatchlings scurry across the sand and into the sea. They must hide because their shells are soft and do not protect them.

_____

2. A day and a half after they hatch, these little ones can find food and even swim. They can't fly yet, but their feathers grow in quickly.

_____

3. This baby stands up within an hour of being born. It might be 6 feet (1.8 m) tall.

_____

4. This baby cannot do much for himself. He won't walk for about a year, so his parents carry him.

_____

Hunting Together for Food

Define It!

carnivore: a meat eater

herd: a group of animals that keep together

prey: an animal hunted for food

pride: a group of lions

Concepts:

Being part of a group helps animals obtain food.

Lions live in a group and hunt together.

Animals often live together in groups so they can help each other find food. Lions are a good example of this because they live in large families called **prides**. A pride might have 10 or 12 lions. Because they are **carnivores**, or meat eaters, lions must hunt for their food. Most of their **prey** can run faster than lions do. So lions work together to catch their prey. One mother lion circles a **herd** of zebras and hides in the tall grass. Another lion sneaks up close to the herd and then runs at a zebra. The frightened zebra runs toward the hiding lion. The lion comes out of hiding, jumps on the zebra, and brings it to the ground. Everyone in the pride shares the meat.

Animal Groups

Circle *true* or *false*.

1. Lions hunt because they are carnivores.   **true**   **false**

2. Lions work together when they hunt.   **true**   **false**

3. Most of their prey cannot run as fast lions do.   **true**   **false**

Animal Groups

Guarding the Group

Define It!

attack: to move against with force

charge: to rush forward

rumbling: a long, low, heavy sound

trumpeting: a loud sound like a trumpet

African elephants travel in a herd. All of the elephants in the herd take care of each other. The leader of the herd is an old mother elephant. The other elephants follow her because she knows how to guard the family if danger appears.

Elephants talk to each other with sounds. Some sounds are so deep and **rumbling** that people cannot hear them. If danger comes near, the rumbling stops. Everyone is on guard. Mothers flap their ears to call their babies to them. The elephants circle around the baby elephants to guard them.

If a lion suddenly **attacks**, the elephants make **trumpeting** sounds and hit the ground with their trunks. The leader puts herself in front of the herd. She flaps her ears out to make herself look even larger. Then she lowers her head and **charges** the enemy in a big cloud of dust.

Write the missing words.

1. Elephants in a _____ take care of each other.

2. Elephants make _____ and _____ sounds.

3. The leader guards the herd from _____.

Life Science: Cycles

Skill Sharpeners—Science • EMC 5323 • © Evan-Moor Corp.

Flocking Together

Define It!

flock: a group of birds together

habitat: a natural home

migrate: to move from one habitat to another

raft: a group of ducks on water

wedge: birds flying in a V-shape

Concepts:

Being part of a group helps animals obtain food and cope with changes in their habitat.

Birds migrate in order to find a habitat with abundant food.

Have you ever seen a **raft** of ducks swimming or a **wedge** of geese flying? Those are names for **flocks** of birds. Why do birds flock together? Some birds feed in a group because it is easier to find food. If one bird finds food, all can feed on it.

Sometimes birds flock together when their **habitat** changes. When the seasons change from summer to fall, the berries, seeds, and bugs that birds eat are harder to find. So birds **migrate** south to warmer places that have more food. Geese, ducks, and swans fly together in a **wedge**, or V-shape, when they migrate. They honk to let each other know where they are. Even at night or in cloudy skies, they can keep together.

1. Why do some birds migrate?

   _____

2. How does a wedge of geese talk to each other?

   _____

Animal Groups

Migrating Monarchs

Monarch butterflies migrate to find food. In the fall, swarms of monarchs migrate from places in the U.S. They come together in Texas and continue on to Mexico. The key shows symbols for dates. The map shows where the butterflies are on those dates.

Read the map and key. Then answer the questions.

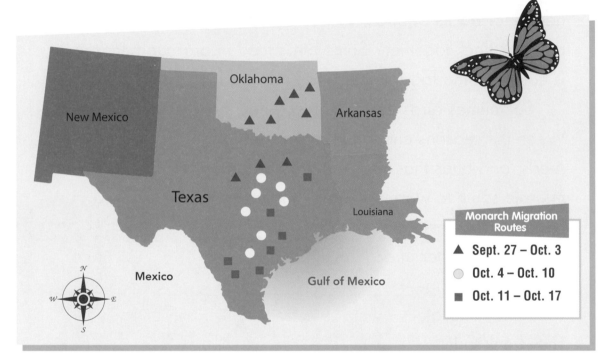

1. In which direction are the monarchs traveling? How do you know? _____

_____

_____

2. What country are the butterflies likely to reach by October 31? _____

3. If the butterflies fly 100 miles (161 km) a day and have to travel 3,000 miles (4,830 km), how long will the trip take them? _____

Life Science: Cycles

Skill Sharpeners—Science • EMC 5323 • © Evan-Moor Corp.

Animal Groups Crossword Puzzle

Use the vocabulary words to complete the crossword puzzle.

habitat   carnivore   charge   pride   prey
trumpeting   rumbling   flock   migrate

Across

2. an animal hunted for food

5. to rush forward

6. a long, low, heavy sound

7. to move from one habitat to another

9. a meat eater

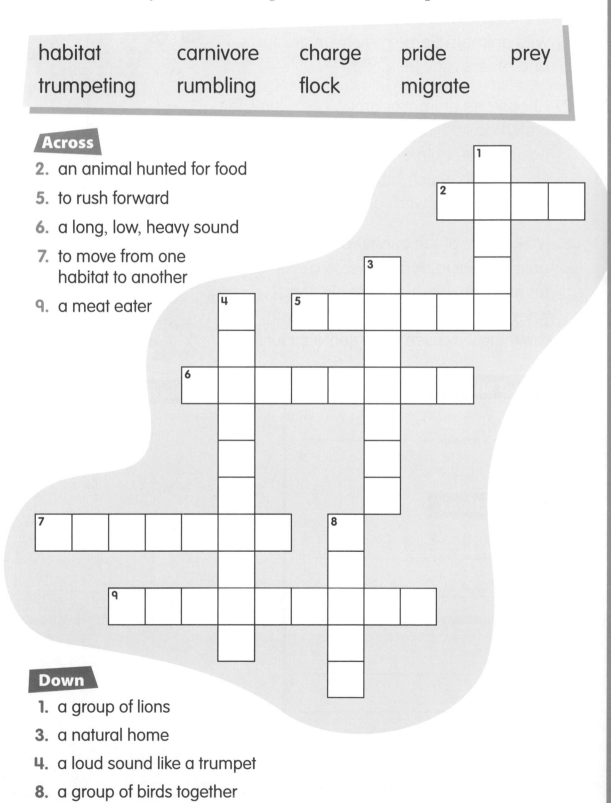

Down

1. a group of lions

3. a natural home

4. a loud sound like a trumpet

8. a group of birds together

Animal Groups

Skills:

Observe, collect, and record information using tools such as a camera and notebook.

Looking at Animals

1. What kinds of animals live where you live? Some may be pets. Some may be wild animals. Some may be in groups, and others may be alone.

2. Choose an animal or group of animals to watch closely. You can go for a walk with an adult to see animals in your neighborhood. Or, you can watch your own pet at home. Take a camera with you.

3. Make a list of the things you see the animals doing. Are they eating? Looking for food? Building a home? Resting? Keeping away from danger? List all the things you see. Take some pictures.

Animal Name

_____

Animal Actions

_____

_____

_____

_____

_____

_____

Animal Drawing or Photo

Animal Groups

A Herd of Elephants

Skills:

Read diagrams and follow a sequence of directions to complete a project.

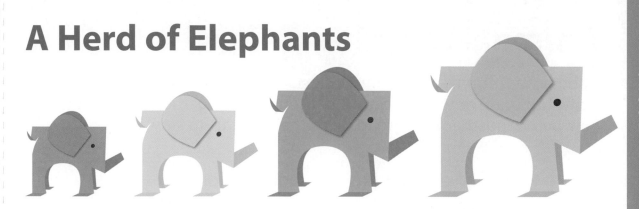

What You Need

- colorful paper 5 ½" x 10" (14 x 25 cm)
- black marker
- scissors
- glue

What You Do

1. Fold the paper in half.

2. Cut a slanted line for the trunk. Cut out a rounded section for the legs.

3. Use the rounded scraps as ears. Fold up the trunk and glue it in place. Cut a tail.

4. Bend up the tail. Fold up the sections for the feet. Add the eyes with the marker.

5. If you wish, make a herd of elephants of different sizes.

Animal Groups

Skills:

Explain how being part of a group helps animals obtain food, defend themselves, and cope with changes.

Use information gained from words and illustrations to demonstrate understanding of text.

Animals Together

Choose an animal group from the list, or use one of your own ideas. Draw a picture of what the animal group does together. Then explain how being together in a group helps the animals to stay alive.

herd of elephants	pride of lions
flock of birds	swarm of butterflies

Draw

1. Name of animal group:

_____

2. Explain what the group does that helps the animals stay alive.

_____

_____

_____

_____

_____

Animal Groups

How Young Animals Survive

Define It!

cub: a young bear

female: able to lay eggs or give birth to young

offspring: the young of an animal

sow: an adult female bear

survive: to stay alive

Animal babies are called **offspring**. The offspring of some animals must **survive** on their own. For example, the parents of a baby turtle, or turtle hatchling, are not around to keep it safe from bigger animals. **Female** turtles lay hundreds of eggs, but only some offspring will survive.

A black bear has fewer offspring. A female black bear, or **sow**, gives birth to two or three **cubs** in the middle of winter. The cubs are ready to leave their warm den in the spring. But the cubs stay close to their mother. She keeps them safe and teaches them to climb a tree quickly to get out of danger. The sow shows her cubs which plants, berries, and insects to eat. When the cubs are one and a half years old, they leave their mother to survive on their own.

offspring

Write the answer to each question.

1. Many turtle hatchlings do not survive. Why? _____

   _____

2. How long do black bear cubs
   live with their mother? _____

Concepts:

Different organisms vary in how they look and function because they have different inherited information.

Some inherited traits appear as an animal grows.

Parents and Offspring

Young animals grow up to **resemble**, or look like, their parents. Do you know the fairy tale called "The Ugly Duckling"? In that story, a baby hatches from an egg, but it doesn't look like the mother duck. Later in the story, the baby grows into a beautiful swan. A swan's egg had somehow gotten into a duck's nest! Ducklings grow into ducks and **cygnets** grow into swans.

Offspring **inherit** some of their **traits**, or looks, from each of their parents. Some traits appear as the young animal grows. Compare the traits of the cygnets and the **pen** (mother swan) in this picture.

Write the missing words.

1. The cygnets have fluffy gray feathers. The pen has smooth _____ feathers.

2. The cygnets have a brown beak. The pen has an _____ beak.

Offspring

From Egg to Frog

Define It!

froglet: a tiny frog

gills: body parts of a water animal

hind: at the back

lungs: body parts for breathing air

tadpole: a newly hatched frog

Concepts:

Many traits of an organism are inherited from its parents.

Some inherited traits appear as the animal grows.

Life Cycle of a Frog

1 A mother frog lays her eggs in water. Each tiny egg is in a floating ball of jelly.

2 A tiny **tadpole** pushes out. It has a long tail for swimming and **gills** for breathing.

3 The tadpole eats water plants. It grows **hind** legs and gets bigger.

6 The froglet eats insects and grows into an adult.

5 The tadpole has become a tiny **froglet**. It jumps onto land. The rest of its tail will soon be gone.

4 The tadpole grows **lungs** for breathing, and loses its gills. It also grows front legs.

offspring

Circle *true* or *false*.

1. An adult frog breathes with gills.   **true**   **false**

2. A tadpole eats water plants.   **true**   **false**

3. A tadpole grows legs and starts to lose its tail.   **true**   **false**

Are You My Parent?

Draw a line to match the parent with its offspring. Use the list of traits to help you. Make a check mark by each trait as you make a match.

Did You Know?

Offspring resemble their parents. There are many kinds of apes and monkeys. Most monkeys have tails, while apes do not. The hair, face, coloring, and arms or legs of the animals help to tell them apart, too.

chimpanzee

orangutan

squirrel monkey

Offspring

_____ face	_____ ears	_____ coloring
_____ tail	_____ face	_____ arms
_____ coloring	_____ hair	_____ face

Life Science: Cycles

Review the Words

Read each clue and write the missing word on the lines.

| trait | cygnet | tadpole | cub | hind |

1. A young frog with gills and a tail is a

   ___ ___ ___ ___ ___ ___ ___.

2. The offspring of a swan is a ___ ___ ___ ___ ___.

3. A frog's ___ ___ ___ ___ legs grow before its front legs do.

4. A colorful beak is a ___ ___ ___ ___ ___ of some adult swans.

5. A black bear ___ ___ ___ stays with its mother for one and
   a half years.

Write the letters from the yellow boxes to answer the riddle.

Science Riddle

**What lives in a little house and must
break through the wall to go out?**

a b___b___ c_____k

offspring

My Traits, Your Traits

All living things pass on traits to their offspring. You may share traits with other people in your family. Compare your traits with a family member's. Circle one answer in each column.

Trait		Yours	Mine
Hair Color		dark or light	dark or light
Hair Type		curly or straight	curly or straight
Eye Color		dark or light	dark or light
Handed		left or right	left or right
Freckles		yes or no	yes or no
Dimples		yes or no	yes or no
Tongue Roll in a U-Shape		yes or no	yes or no

offspring

Black Bears Bookmark

Skill:

Follow a sequence of directions to complete a science project.

What You Need

- black construction paper
- brown construction paper
- black marker
- scissors
- glue
- crayons

What You Do

1. Cut a black circle for the mother bear's head.

2. Black bears have a long snout. Cut a brown oval for the snout.

3. Draw the nose and mouth on the snout, then glue it to the head.

4. Draw two eyes near the snout.

5. Black bears have longer ears than some other bears do. Cut two ears from black paper. Glue them on.

6. Glue the mother bear near the bottom of a brown rectangle. Cut a paw from black paper and glue it on. Draw claws.

7. Follow the same steps to make a smaller bear cub for the top of the tree.

8. Draw the tree trunk details with crayon.

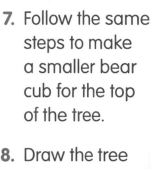

offspring

Life Science: Cycles

It's a Frog's Life

Write a story telling how it feels to be a tadpole who wants to be a frog. Tell how the tadpole feels as it grows up. Give your story a title.

Hint

How is a tadpole different from its parents? It lives in water, not on land. It has gills, not lungs. It has a tail. A tadpole eats plants.

Skills:

Apply scientific knowledge to write a narrative about an imagined experience.

Use descriptive details and clear event sequences.

Use words and phrases to signal event order (e.g., *at first, then, at last*).

Offspring

_____

_____

_____

_____

_____

_____

_____

_____

_____

_____

_____

_____

_____

Fossils

A **fossil** is the remains or marks of a plant or an animal that lived long ago. Living things **decay** when they die. But if their bones, shells, or teeth are buried quickly by **sediment**, a fossil can form. Over millions of years, heavy layers of sediment pile up and harden into rock.

A *mold* is one kind of fossil. It is made when a plant or an animal rots away and leaves only its shape in the rock.

A *cast* is another kind of fossil. It is made when **minerals** fill a mold in the same shape as the plant or animal.

A *trace fossil* is made from things such as footprints or nests. They tell scientists how the animals moved and lived.

Define It!

decay: to break down or rot

fossil: remains or marks of a living thing that lived long ago

mineral: something found in nature that is not plant or animal

sediment: soil or sand that forms layers on land or under water

mold

cast

dinosaur's footprint

Concepts:

Fossils provide evidence about the types of organisms that lived long ago.

Types of fossils include molds, casts, and trace fossils.

Check the box that answers the question.

1. Which of these would **not** make a trace fossil?

   ☐ footprint   ☐ bone   ☐ nest

2. Which of these could show the entire shape of an animal?

   ☐ sediment   ☐ trace fossil   ☐ cast

Fossils

The Fossil Record

Define It!

extinct: no longer to be found living

fossil record: the history of life on Earth as told by fossils

marker fossil: fossil that marks a time in the fossil record

trilobite: an extinct sea animal

The layers of rock on Earth have built up over time. Scientists try to understand what Earth was like long ago by studying fossils in the different layers of rock. Scientists call Earth's layers of rock the **fossil record**.

Trilobite fossils are common in the fossil record. Trilobites were sea animals that lived about 250 million to 540 million years ago. They are now **extinct**, or no longer to be found. These extinct animals are useful to scientists today. Trilobites are **marker fossils**. When a new kind of fossil is discovered, scientists want to figure out when that plant or animal lived. The fossil record can tell scientists if the organism lived before, after, or at the same time as trilobites.

Write the missing words.

1. Trilobites are _____ sea animals that had three main body parts.

2. The layers of rock in the _____ give clues about when an organism lived.

Fossils

Earth's Past

Define It!

continents: the seven largest bodies of land on Earth

fern: a feathery plant

landmass: a large body of land

Concepts:

We learn about Earth's early environments from fossils of plants and animals that lived long ago.

Some changes in Earth's surface happen slowly over millions of years.

The story of Earth's past tells of big changes over millions of years. Fossils are clues that tell how life on Earth changed over time. Fossils of a **fern** plant gave scientists a clue. The same fossils were found on different **continents**. The scientists began to think that the continents were once connected. Now scientists think that all the continents were one giant **landmass** about 200 million years ago. They call that landmass Pangaea (pan-JEE-uh).

Today, millions of years after Pangaea broke apart, the continents are still moving very slowly. The movement of continents builds mountains. When two continents push into each other, their rock layers push together and make a mountain. Sometimes the layers are pushed up all the way from the ocean floor. If those rock layers hold fossils, the fossils travel up with the rocks. This is why fossils of sea animals have been found at the tops of mountains.

Circle *true* or *false*.

1. Earth has always looked the way it does now.   **true**   **false**

2. Fossils can tell us what Earth looked like long ago.   **true**   **false**

3. Sea animal fossils cannot be found on a mountain.   **true**   **false**

Stuck in Time

Scientists have been digging up thousands of fossils in the city of Los Angeles, California! The area is called the La Brea (lah BRAY-uh) Tar Pits. Scientists have found the bones of mammoths and saber-toothed cats there. These extinct animals were trapped in the tar pits about 30,000 years ago.

Write the letter of the sentence that matches each picture.

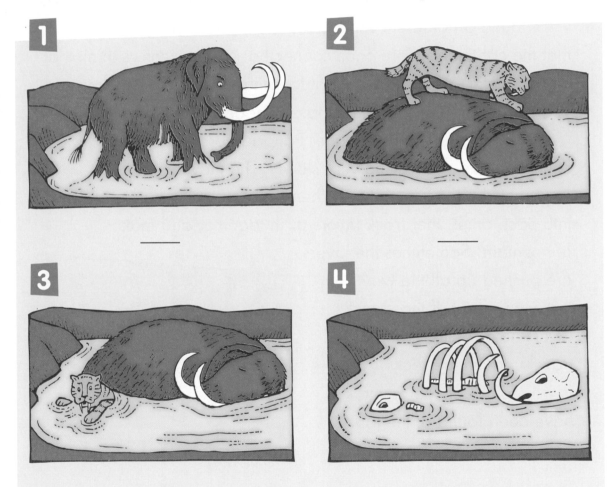

a. A hungry saber-toothed cat attacked the mammoth.

b. Over time, both animals were buried in the tar pit.

c. A mammoth wandered into a pool of sticky tar.

d. The saber-toothed cat was stuck, and died of hunger.

Fossils Crossword Puzzle

Use the vocabulary words to complete the crossword puzzle.

| decay | fossil | trilobite | landmass |
| continents | extinct | sediment | fern |

Across

4. the seven largest bodies of land on Earth
6. soil or sand that forms layers on land or underwater
8. no longer found to be living

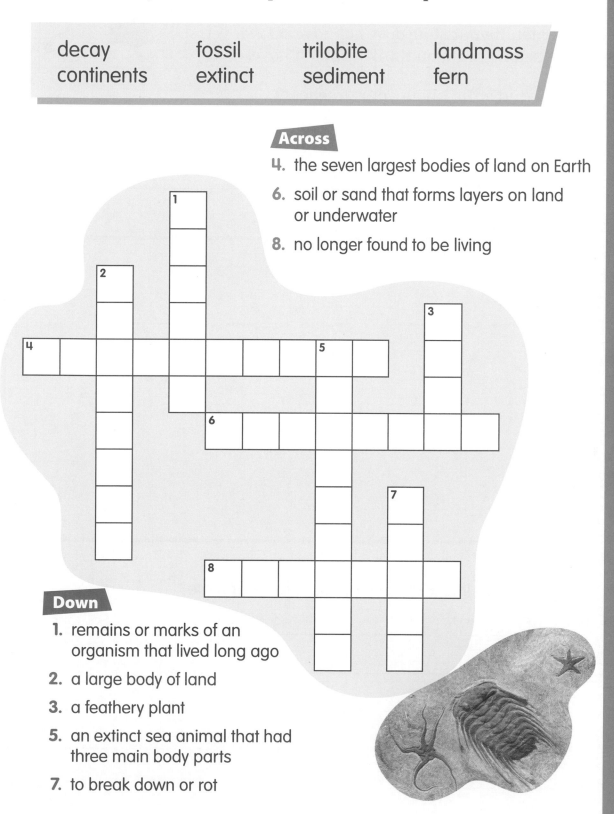

Down

1. remains or marks of an organism that lived long ago
2. a large body of land
3. a feathery plant
5. an extinct sea animal that had three main body parts
7. to break down or rot

Fossils

Skills:

Conduct research on a science topic and write an illustrated report.

My State's Fossil

Most U.S. states have chosen a state fossil. Look for your state's fossil in a library book or on the Internet. If your state does not have a fossil yet, choose one that you think it should have.

Draw and write about your state fossil.

My State: _____

My State's Fossil: _____

Draw

_____
_____
_____
_____
_____
_____

What makes this fossil a good fossil for your state?

_____
_____
_____
_____
_____

Fossils

Make Your Own Fossil

Skill:

Follow a sequence of directions to complete a science project.

What You Need

- petroleum jelly
- plaster of Paris
- water
- bowl and spoon
- cardboard
- leaves and shells

What You Do

1. Coat a leaf and a shell with petroleum jelly. Set them aside.

2. Follow the directions to mix the plaster and the water. Have an adult help you.

3. Spread some plaster on the cardboard. Use enough plaster so that you can press the leaf and the shell into it.

4. Press the coated leaf and shell gently into the plaster. Try not to move them once they are in the plaster.

5. Let the plaster dry overnight. When it is dry, carefully remove the leaf and the shell.

Fossils

Skill:

Apply scientific knowledge to write a narrative about an imagined experience.

Fossil Discovery

Pretend that you are a shell fossil. You are the remains of an extinct sea animal. Tell the story of how you came to be at the top of a mountain.

Hint

Layers of sediment built up on the ocean floor for millions of years. When the layers were pushed up by the moving continents, they became mountains.

_____

_____

_____

_____

_____

_____

_____

_____

The Dinosaurs

Concepts:

Some kinds of animals that once lived on Earth are no longer found anywhere.

Dinosaurs had bodies that were built to help them survive.

Dinosaurs were **reptiles** that lived on Earth long ago for about 160 million years. How did they **survive** for so long?

One answer is that their bodies were built to help them survive. Meat-eating dinosaurs like *Tyrannosaurus rex* (tuh-RAN-no-SOHR-uhs reks) had two short legs in front. They traveled on their two **hind** legs. Meat eaters had big jaws and sharp teeth. They had hands with sharp claws to catch and hold their **prey**.

Some plant-eating dinosaurs were giants. *Diplodocus* (deh-PLAH-duh-kuhs) was about 90 feet (27 m) long, with a small head and a long neck. These dinosaurs moved on four feet because of their large size. Their size could scare away meat-eating dinosaurs.

Other plant-eating dinosaurs had **armor** to protect them. They had bony plates, horns, and spikes. *Triceratops* had head armor. *Stegosaurus* (STEG-uh-SOHR-uhs) could swing its spiked tail to strike an enemy.

Tyrannosaurus rex (T. rex)

Diplodocus

Stegosaurus

Write the missing words.

1. Meat-eating dinosaurs had big jaws and _____.

2. Some plant-eating dinosaurs had _____ such as bony plates, horns, and spikes.

Dinosaurs

Concept:

The fossil record provides evidence about dinosaurs and their disappearance.

Dinosaurs Disappear

Define It!

asteroid: a small rocky body that travels around the sun

crater: a bowl-shaped hole

fossil record: layers of rock containing fossils

Although dinosaurs were the main form of animal life for millions of years, they died out about 65 million years ago. We know this because there are no dinosaur fossils in the **fossil record** after that time. What happened that caused the dinosaurs to disappear? Scientists have been asking that same question.

One idea is that a large space rock, called an **asteroid**, hit Earth. Today in Mexico there is a giant hole more than 100 miles (161 km) across. Scientists think an asteroid made this **crater**. When the asteroid hit Earth, it caused large amounts of dust to rise into the air. It started huge fires, too. The smoke and dust blocked out the sun. Plants could not live without sunlight. Plant-eating dinosaurs could not live without plants. And meat eaters died when their prey were gone.

Answer each question.

1. When did the dinosaurs die out? _____

2. What made a huge crater in Mexico? _____

3. Without the sun, living things _____.

Dinosaur Hunters

Define It!

ancient: belonging to times long past

paleontologist: a scientist who studies rocks and fossils to learn about living things of the past

Concepts:

Fossils provide evidence about organisms that lived long ago.

A paleontologist is a scientist who studies living things of the ancient past.

Dinosaurs lived long before people did. About 200 years ago, people did not know about dinosaurs and their **ancient** world. If fossils were found, people did not know what they were. Then, in the early 1800s, science-minded people started to look at fossils differently. Scientists began to think that the large teeth and bones they found belonged to a new kind of animal. In 1842, Sir Richard Owen named the new group of animals *dinosaurs*, which means "terrible lizards." Dinosaurs were not lizards, but the name *dinosaur* has stuck. A new science was born that studied living things of long ago. Today, scientists called **paleontologists** (PAY-lee-ahn-TAHL-uh-jists) are using rocks and fossils to learn more about living things of the ancient past.

Triceratops

Dinosaurs

Circle *true* or *false*.

1. Dinosaurs lived until the 1800s.   true   false

2. Dinosaurs were giant lizards.   true   false

3. Paleontologists study the ancient past.   true   false

Skills:

Analyze and interpret information presented in an illustration.

Gather and record scientific data in a table or chart.

Bird or Dinosaur?

Many scientists think that birds are modern-day relatives of dinosaurs. The scientists see many things about the bodies of birds and dinosaurs that are alike. For example, scientists think that *Tyrannosaurus rex* ran on its toes, just as many birds do.

Compare the pictures of a dinosaur's foot and a bird's foot. Write your data in the chart.

Tyrannosaurus Rex

Bird

Question	Tyrannosaurus Rex	Bird
1. How many toes in front?		
2. How many toes in back?		
3. How many toes have claws?		

Life Science: Changes

Skill Sharpeners—Science • EMC 5323 • © Evan-Moor Corp.

Either/Or Questions

Write each answer.

1. Is something that is ancient new **or** old? _____

2. Is prey an animal that hunts **or** one that
   is hunted? _____

3. Is armor hard **or** soft? _____

4. Is an asteroid an animal **or** a rock? _____

5. Is a paleontologist a person **or** a dinosaur? _____

6. Is a crater a hole **or** an asteroid? _____

7. Is a hind leg in front **or** in back? _____

8. Have birds survived **or** died out? _____

9. Was a dinosaur a reptile **or** a mammal? _____

Dinosaurs

Life Science: Changes

Skills:

Conduct a survey to gather data and construct a bar graph.

Dinosaur Question

Ask six family members or friends this question: *Which one of these dinosaurs do you like best?* Make a tally of their answers in the boxes below the pictures. Then color the bar graph to show the results of your survey.

Question: Which one of these dinosaurs do you like best?

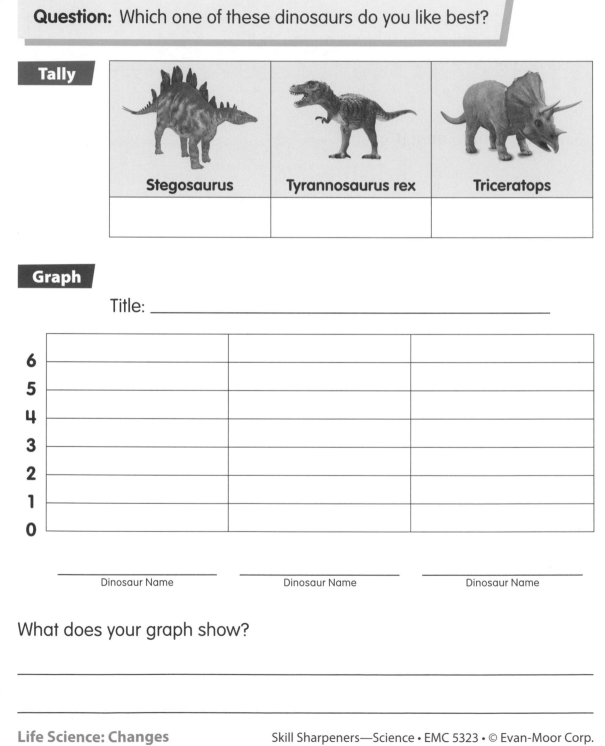

Tally

Stegosaurus	Tyrannosaurus rex	Triceratops

Graph

Title: _____

6			
5			
4			
3			
2			
1			
0			

_____ _____ _____
Dinosaur Name   Dinosaur Name   Dinosaur Name

What does your graph show?

_____

_____

Torn-Paper Dinosaur Fossil

Skill:

Follow a sequence of directions to complete a science project.

What You Need

- a picture of a dinosaur fossil from a book or the Internet

- construction paper (black, brown)

- glue

What You Do

1. Choose a picture of a dinosaur fossil. It can be all or part of a skeleton, such as a skull or a foot. You will be making a torn-paper picture like it. Don't worry, you don't have to make a perfect copy! This picture is the spark for your own ideas.

2. Use a sheet of black paper for the background.

3. Tear the brown paper to form the shapes of the bones of the dinosaur skeleton. If you like, you can first draw the shapes lightly with pencil and then tear them. (A good way to tear paper is to carefully pinch and pull it.)

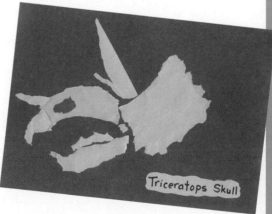

Triceratops Skull

4. Glue the bones on the black paper to form the dinosaur fossil.

5. Make a title for your picture, using the name of the dinosaur.

Dinosaurs

My Dinosaur

Skills:

Draw some observable features of a dinosaur fossil.

Recall or gather information from print or digital sources.

Write explanatory text.

Wow!

Bucky Derflinger found his first dinosaur fossil on his family's ranch when he was only 8 years old. When he was 20 years old, he found a *Tyrannosaurus rex* there. Its name is Bucky, and it is in a museum.

Using a picture from a book or the Internet, draw the skeleton of the kind of dinosaur you would most like to find. Then write about the dinosaur and tell why you find it interesting.

Draw

Someday, I would like to find a

_____

_____

_____

_____

_____

Life Science: Changes

Concept:

External characteristics of living things allow their needs to be met.

Dolphin Adaptations

Living things have **traits**, or features. A trait that helps a living thing **survive** is called an **adaptation**. Dolphins have a special adaptation that helps them breathe underwater. A dolphin breathes through a **blowhole** on the top of its head, instead of through a nose or mouth like ours. The dolphin uses strong muscles to open its blowhole when it swims to the water's surface. As it dives underwater, the blowhole closes.

Dolphins have other adaptations, too. They have a tail and two flippers. They swim through the water by moving their tail and steering with their flippers.

Define It!

adaptation: a feature that helps a living thing stay alive

blowhole: an opening on the top of the head used for breathing

survive: to stay alive

trait: a feature belonging to a living thing

Explain how a dolphin uses each adaptation.

1. blowhole _____

2. tail _____

3. flipper _____

Rock Pocket Mouse

Color is an adaptation that helps animals survive. When animals hide by blending in with the things around them, it is called **camouflage**. The rock pocket mouse is an example of camouflage. This mouse lived in the desert. Its sandy-brown color blended in with the sand and rocks and camouflaged the mouse. Owls and other animals that eat mice couldn't easily see it, so the rock pocket mice had a good chance of surviving. Then, long ago, **lava** from a **volcano** flowed over part of the desert. The lava cooled into dark rock. The light-colored mice were no longer safe on the dark rocks. By chance, a few dark-colored mice were born. The dark-colored mice survived, and the light-colored mice were eaten. More dark mice were born. Now, almost all of the rock pocket mice living on the dark rocks are dark-colored. And the mice living in the sandy part of the desert are light-colored.

photo by Roger W. Barbour

photo by R. B. Forbes.
© American Society of Mammalogists

Answer the questions.

1. How does the rock pocket mouse hide? _____

2. Which mice survive on the dark rocks?

_____

Adaptations

Cactus Spines

Concepts:

Living things have characteristics that allow them to survive.

Living things have different characteristics that allow their needs to be met.

A cactus has adaptations that help it survive in a hot, dry desert. One adaptation is its needles, or **spines**. A spine is an adaptation of a leaf. Spines can be useful in different ways. Spines catch water and drip it toward the roots of the cactus. A cactus may be thickly covered with spines that shade it and keep it from drying out in the sun. Some spines **protect** a cactus from animals looking for a juicy meal. The animals learn that the spines will stick in their mouth, so they keep away. The jumping cholla (CHOY-ah) cactus uses its spines to **reproduce**. If an animal brushes against a jumping cholla, a small piece breaks off and sticks to the animal. In time, the piece drops to the ground, grows roots, and becomes a new plant.

Circle *true* or *false*.

1. A cactus spine adapted from a leaf.   **true**   **false**

2. Spines are not very useful to a cactus.   **true**   **false**

3. One type of cactus uses its spines to make
   new plants.   **true**   **false**

Adaptations

Barrel Cactus

Skills:

Identify the external characteristics of different kinds of plants and animals that allow their needs to be met.

Analyze and interpret information presented in a visual format.

Cactus spines catch water to help a cactus survive. The barrel cactus has other adaptations that help it get and store water. The roots of the cactus spread out like a net to quickly drink up even the smallest amount of desert rain. A barrel cactus has folds that can swell and store gallons or liters of water. Its thick, waxy skin keeps the water inside the plant from escaping into the air.

Label the diagram to show four adaptations of the barrel cactus. Use the words below.

roots   folds   spines   thick, waxy skin

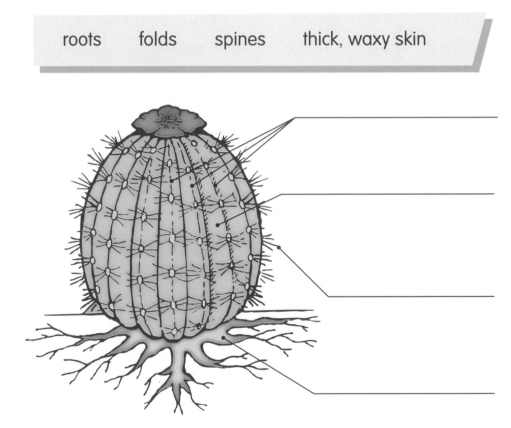

Complete each sentence to describe the adaptation.

1. When rain falls in the desert, it dries up quickly. That is why the roots

_____

2. A cactus may have to live without rain for a long time. That is why

   the folds _____

Review the Words

Skill:

Apply content vocabulary in context sentences.

Read each clue and write the missing word on the lines.

| camouflage | volcano | adaptation |
| blowhole | spines | survive |

1. A dolphin breathes through its

___ ___ ___ ___ ___ ___ ___ .

2. The dark color of a rock pocket mouse is an

___ ___ ___ ___ ___ ___ ___ ___ ___ ___ .

3. The sharp needles of a cactus are called

___ ___ ___ ___ ___ ___ .

4. Adaptations help living things ___ ___ ___ ___ ___ ___ ___ .

5. Animals use ___ ___ ___ ___ ___ ___ ___ ___ ___ ___
to help them hide.

6. Lava flows from a ___ ___ ___ ___ ___ ___ ___ .

Write the letters from the yellow boxes to answer the riddle.

Science Riddle

What is a mouse's favorite game?

___ ___ de and ___ q ___ ___ ___ k

Life Science: Changes

Adaptations

Plant Adaptation

Skills:

Gather and interpret scientific data from observation.

Use observations to construct an explanation.

A cactus can store water for months. But not all plants have this adaptation. See what happens to a celery stalk with and without water.

What You Need

- celery stalk
- paper towel
- water in a glass
- an adult to cut the celery

What You Do

1. Have an adult cut off the bottom of the celery stalk. Notice the tiny holes at the bottom. These are tiny tubes that go up the stalk.

2. Set the stalk on a paper towel and leave it out overnight.

3. Look at the celery stalk. Notice how it looks and feels now.

4. Stand the celery in the glass of water, with the cut end at the bottom. Leave it like this overnight.

5. Now look at the celery stalk. Notice how it looks and feels.

What Did You Discover?

1. Describe how the celery looked and felt after being on the paper towel.

_____

2. Describe how the celery looked and felt after being in water overnight.

_____

3. Compare the celery with a cactus. Write one way they are alike and one way they are different.

_____

_____

Adaptations

Camouflage Collage

What You Need

- construction paper (orange or tan, blue, green, red, yellow)
- scissors
- glue
- marker

Skills:

Represent the natural world using models.

Follow a sequence of instructions to complete a science project.

What You Do

1. Use a sheet of blue paper for the background. Cut orange or tan paper for the desert and glue it to the blue background.

2. Make a mouse from the same color (orange or tan) paper. Cut a half circle for the body.

3. Cut two small circles for ears.

4. To make a curly tail, cut out a small circle. Then cut out the center of the small circle and use the scrap for the tail.

5. Glue the ears and tail to the body.

6. Draw the mouse's face.

fold

7. To make the mouse pop out of the picture, cut two small strips of paper and accordion-fold them. Glue one end of the folded tabs to the back of the mouse. Then glue the other ends to the desert.

8. Add a bright sun and some cactuses to your desert picture.

Adaptations

Skills:

Write explanatory text to convey information clearly.

Explain the characteristics that help a living thing survive.

What's My Adaptation?

Pretend that you are a dolphin, a rock pocket mouse, or a cactus. Explain what your adaptations are and how they help you survive. Then draw and label a diagram that shows your adaptations.

Hint

Dolphins have adapted to living underwater. The rock pocket mouse has adapted to the color of the dark rocks. Cactus plants have adapted to living in a hot, dry desert.

_____

_____

_____

_____

_____

Draw

Iguana in the Ocean

Define It!

affect: to make a difference to

algae: tiny water plants

ecosystem: a community of living and nonliving things that have an effect on each other

habitat: a home in nature

iguana: a type of lizard

Concepts:

Ecosystems include living and nonliving things that interact with each other.

Nonliving things can make changes in a habitat that affect the living things there.

An **ecosystem** is made up of nonliving and living things in their **habitats**. When one thing changes, it **affects** the others.

The Galápagos (guh-LAH-puh-gohs) Islands are a special ecosystem because many of the animals that live there are not found anywhere else. One such animal is a lizard called the Galápagos **iguana**. All lizards are land animals except for these iguanas. They swim into the ocean to eat tiny **algae** that grow there. Then they return to land to warm up in the sun. During some years, the ocean gets warmer and there is less algae to eat. When this happens, the iguanas are affected. The bones in their bodies shrink in size. Their smaller bodies warm up in the sun more quickly, so they can make more trips to feed in the water. When the ocean gets colder again, the iguanas grow larger.

Answer the questions.

1. What happens in the iguana's habitat that changes its food supply?

   _____

2. How do the iguanas change? _____

Ecosystems

Concepts:

Humans have unintentionally changed some ecosystems by bringing in other species.

A living thing can make changes in a habitat that affect the organisms living there.

Brown Tree Snakes

Without knowing it, people changed the ecosystem on the island of Guam (gwahm). Brown tree snakes slipped in more than 60 years ago. They were hiding in the wheels of **military** planes and on **cargo** boats. Now there are more than two million brown tree snakes on Guam. The snakes have caused big changes to the ecosystem. There used to be many forest birds, but the snakes ate them. Now birds are nearly all gone, and some **species** of birds are **extinct**. Because there are fewer birds to eat spiders, there are many more spiders. There are not enough birds to help spread seeds, so fewer new trees and plants grow in the forest. Scientists are working to find ways to get rid of the snakes without harming other parts of the ecosystem.

Define It!

cargo: goods carried on a ship

extinct: no longer to be found living

military: armed forces

species: a group of plants or animals that has many common traits

Circle *true* or *false*.

1. There are millions of snakes on Guam.   **true**   **false**

2. Birds are nearly gone from Guam.   **true**   **false**

3. Spiders are extinct species on Guam.   **true**   **false**

Ecosystems

Paperbark Trees

Concepts:

Humans have deliberately changed ecosystems by bringing in other species.

New species in an ecosystem can affect the survival of native plants and animals.

People brought paperbark trees from Australia to Florida, and the trees changed Florida's ecosystem. People planted the trees in Florida in the 1880s, hoping the trees could help dry out swampy land. But the paperbark trees took over, blocking out light and making it impossible for Florida's **native** plants to grow. Without the native plants, many animal and insect species could not survive. Unfortunately, very few animal species can live in the paperbark tree's habitat.

Another problem is that the trees **survive** Florida's **wildfires** but Florida's native plants do not. So, there are fewer native plants and more paperbark trees. It is a very big problem to **control** the spread of these trees. Scientists know that this tree changes the ecosystem in Florida and makes native plant and animal species disappear.

Answer the questions.

1. Why are Florida's native plants important? _____

   _____

2. What problem do scientists have? _____

   _____

Ecosystems

Skills:

Read and interpret data from a bar graph.

Solve single-step problems using information presented in a bar graph.

Birds on the Move

Earth changes are happening. As Earth grows warmer, the ecosystems in which birds find food are changing, too. For forty years, scientists kept track of where birds live. By 2010, the habitats of birds in America had moved north. This graph shows the distance in miles and kilometers.

Look at the graph and answer the questions.

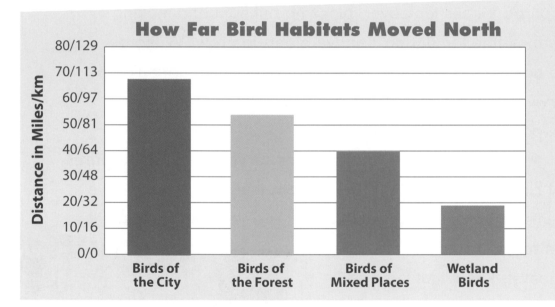

1. Which type of bird had to move the greatest distance to find food?

   _____

2. Which type of bird had to move about 54 miles (87 km) to the north?

   _____

3. How many miles/kilometers did birds of mixed places have to move?

   _____

4. Which birds moved fewer than 20 miles (32 km)?

   _____

Life Science: Changes

Ecosystems

Ecosystems Crossword Puzzle

Use the vocabulary words to complete the crossword puzzle.

iguana	species	native	ecosystem
wildfire	affect	extinct	algae

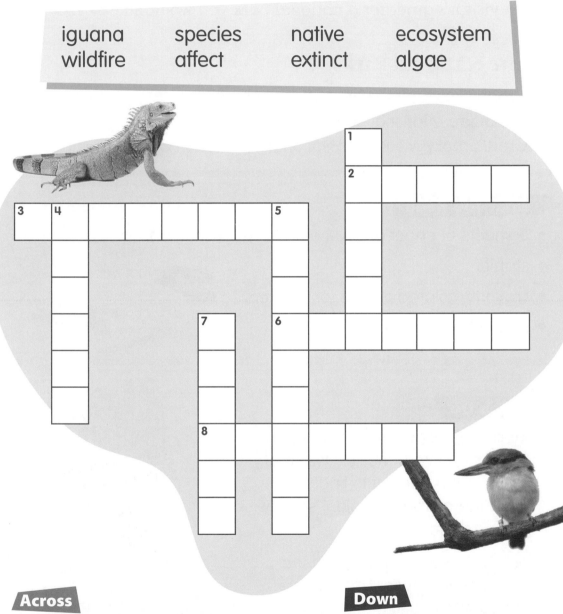

Across

2. tiny water plants
3. a fire that destroys a wide area
6. a group of plants or animals that has many common traits
8. no longer to be found living

Down

1. belonging to a place
4. a type of lizard
5. a community of living and nonliving things
7. to make a difference to

Ecosystems

Hands-on Activity

Skills:

Conduct research on a science topic and write a report in the form of a national parks visitor's guide.

Ecosystem Visitor's Guide

National parks take care of many types of ecosystems. People visit national parks to see mountains, wetlands, deserts, and forests. Make a visitor's guide for a national park you would like to visit.

Some National Parks

- Grand Canyon National Park (Arizona)
- Everglades National Park (Florida)
- Great Smoky Mountains National Park (North Carolina/Tennessee)

What You Need

- 5 sheets of paper and 1 sheet of construction paper
- stapler
- crayons, colored pencils, or markers
- library books or the Internet

What You Do

1. Choose a national park from the list or one of your choice. Use library books or the Internet to find out about the animal and plant species that live there.

2. Fold the sheets of paper and the construction paper in half. Staple them at the fold to make a book.

3. On each page of your visitor's guide, draw or show a picture of a plant or an animal that lives in the park.

4. Write the name of the organism and tell something about its ecosystem.

Ecosystems

88

Life Science: Changes

Skill Sharpeners—Science • EMC 5323 • © Evan-Moor Corp.

Galápagos Paper Mosaic

What You Need

- construction paper (blue, black, brown or tan, green, and other colors)
- scissors
- pencil
- glue
- iguana picture, page 83

Skills:

Apply observation skills to create a paper mosaic.

Follow a sequence of directions to complete a science project.

What You Do

1. Trim a half sheet of blue paper for the ocean and glue it to a sheet of tan or brown paper. This will make the land and ocean.

2. With a pencil, lightly draw a large, simple outline of an iguana. Show that this iguana lives both on land and in the sea. Use the picture on page 83 to spark your ideas.

3. Cut small squares of colored paper. Fill in each area of the iguana by gluing on the squares. Cut smaller pieces if needed. **Hint:** It is easier and neater to put glue on the background paper rather than on the paper squares.

4. Cut paper triangles and glue them along the iguana's back.

5. Add some green algae in the ocean for the iguana to eat.

6. Add a rock or a crab to the ecosystem if you wish.

Ecosystems

Skills:

Apply observational skills to a familiar ecosystem.

Write informative text to examine a topic and convey ideas and information clearly.

Habitat, Sweet Home

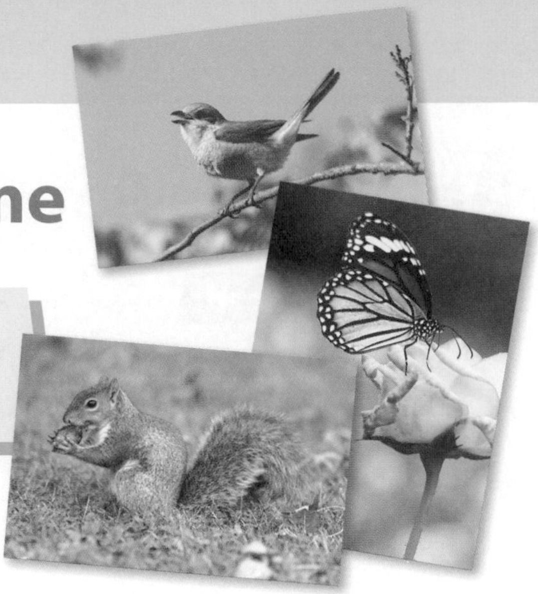

Hint

Ecosystems may have many habitats, or animal homes.

Write a list of the animals you have seen in your neighborhood, such as birds, insects, and mammals.

______________________	______________________
______________________	______________________
______________________	______________________

1. Which animal do you like best?

____

2. What is its habitat?

____

____

3. Draw a picture of the animal in its habitat.

The Atmosphere

Layers of **gases** circle Earth and stretch for hundreds of miles or kilometers above it. These layers are the **atmosphere**. The air we breathe is part of the atmosphere. The atmosphere is where **weather** happens. Weather is what is happening in the atmosphere in a certain place and time. Weather changes as the atmosphere changes.

One of the jobs of the atmosphere is to soak up heat from the sun's rays. It must also let some of the heat go back into space. This is how the atmosphere keeps Earth's **temperatures** from becoming too hot or too cold.

People can't change the weather, but we can measure it. We measure temperature with a **thermometer**. It tells us how hot or cold the air is.

Define It!

atmosphere: layers of gases that circle Earth

gas: matter that is not liquid or solid

temperature: hotness or coldness

thermometer: a tool that measures temperature

weather: what happens in the atmosphere

Concepts:

Earth is surrounded by layers of gases that make up the atmosphere.

Weather happens in the atmosphere.

Circle *true* or *false*.

1. Weather happens in the atmosphere.   true   false

2. The atmosphere does not change.   true   false

3. Temperature can be measured.   true   false

Weather

Precipitation

The atmosphere holds water in the form of **water vapor**. Water vapor is made when water **evaporates**, or changes from a liquid to a gas. The vapor disappears into the air. If water vapor is lifted high enough into the air, it cools. Cooling causes the water vapor to **condense**, or form tiny drops of water. This is how clouds are formed. The tiny drops grow and change inside the clouds until they become so heavy that they fall to the ground as **precipitation**. Rain, snow, sleet, and hail are all types of precipitation. Scientists use a **rain gauge** to measure the rain that falls in a place.

Define It!

condense: to change from a gas to a liquid form

evaporate: to change into a gas

precipitation: water that falls as rain, snow, sleet, or hail

rain gauge: a tool that measures rainfall

water vapor: the gas that clouds are made of

rain   snow

sleet   hail

Answer the questions.

1. How does water get into the air? _____

2. What happens to water vapor when it cools?

_____

Weather

Wind

Meteorologists are scientists who study weather and **predict** its changes. Changes in the weather happen when the wind changes speed and direction. That is why meteorologists use special tools to measure wind speed and direction.

A **wind vane** is a tool that points in the direction the wind is blowing from. Another tool, called an **anemometer** (ann-ih-MOM-uh-tur), is used to measure how fast the wind is blowing. The faster the anemometer spins, the faster the wind is blowing. Without these tools, it would be difficult to measure the wind. It would also be difficult to know how strong a storm is, or to know in which direction it is moving.

Define It!

anemometer: a tool that measures wind speed

meteorologist: a scientist who studies the atmosphere and weather

predict: to say what will happen in the future

wind vane: a tool that shows wind direction

wind vane

anemometer

Write the tool that each person would use.

1. Maria wants to know in which direction the wind is blowing.

   _____

2. Craig wants to measure how fast the wind is blowing.

   _____

3. Rachel wants to know if the wind is traveling east or west.

   _____

Weather

The Water Cycle

This diagram shows how the water on Earth is always moving through the water cycle. A *cycle* is something that repeats over and over. Water evaporates into the air. The water vapor forms clouds. Precipitation falls from the clouds. Then evaporation happens again.

Label the diagram of the water cycle. Use the words below.

land	sun	clouds	ocean	precipitation	evaporation

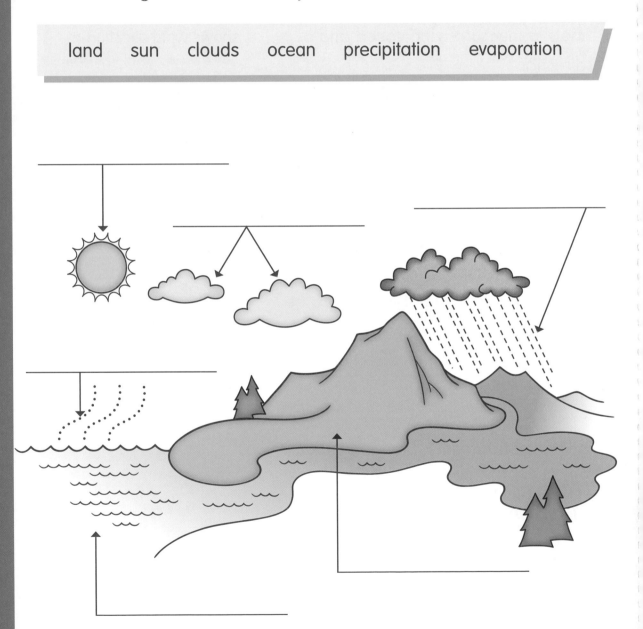

Weather

94

Either/Or Questions

Write each answer.

1. Does temperature tell how warm **or** how wet something is?

_____

2. Is snow atmosphere **or** precipitation?

_____

3. Does an anemometer measure wind speed **or** rainfall?

_____

4. Does a thermometer measure wind direction **or** hot and cold?

_____

5. Does a meteorologist predict the weather **or** study rocks?

_____

6. Is water vapor in the ocean **or** the atmosphere?

_____

7. Can water predict **or** evaporate?

_____

8. Are clouds formed by water vapor **or** a wind vane?

_____

Weather

Skills:

Make observations to gather data and present it in a table.

A Cloud Record

Scientists group clouds into three main types. You can tell each type of cloud by its shape and by how high it is in the atmosphere.

Stratus (STRAY-tuhs)
Stratus clouds are the lowest clouds. They look like a flat gray sheet in the sky. Light rain or snow may fall from stratus clouds. Stratus clouds close to the ground are called *fog.*

Cumulus (KYOO-myuh-luhs)
Cumulus clouds are puffy white clouds, higher than stratus clouds. They mostly bring fair weather. However, they may gather and form huge storm clouds. Those bring thunder, lightning, rain, and hail.

Cirrus (SEAR-uhs)
Cirrus clouds are thin clouds that look feathery. They are the highest clouds in the sky. Cirrus clouds are a sign that the weather may change.

My Cloud Record

Day	Type of Cloud	Weather Today	I Predict Tomorrow Will Be...

Puffy Paint Clouds

Skills:

Follow a sequence of directions to complete an art project.

Demonstrate knowledge of cloud forms.

What You Need

- construction paper (light blue)
- shaving cream
- about 3 tablespoons (44 mL) of white glue
- paintbrush
- small paper cup
- drop of black paint
- marking pens

What You Do

1. Mix the white glue with enough shaving cream to fill the cup. Stir gently with the paintbrush so that the puffy paint will stay puffy.

2. Paint the three main types of clouds down the left side of the paper. Start at the top with feathery cirrus clouds.

3. Next, paint puffy cumulus clouds.

4. Before painting flat gray stratus clouds, add a tiny drop of black paint to the puffy paint to make it gray.

5. Let the puffy paint dry for a day.

6. The next day, label each type of cloud and describe it.

Cirrus
Thin and feathery clouds. They are the highest clouds.

Cumulus
Puffy white clouds, higher than stratus. Bring fair weather.

Stratus
Low clouds, like a flat, gray sheet.

weather

Skills:

Apply scientific knowledge to write a narrative about an imagined experience.

Demonstrate familiarity with the concept of the water cycle.

A Raindrop's Story

Pretend that you are a raindrop that falls to Earth. You make a splash landing in a puddle on the playground. Tell how you got there. Describe your trip through the water cycle.

Hint

In the water cycle, water evaporates from the ocean into the atmosphere. The water vapor is carried up, where it cools and forms clouds. It falls to Earth again as raindrops.

_____

_____

_____

_____

_____

_____

_____

YOU

Skill Sharpeners—Science • EMC 5323 • © Evan-Moor Corp.

Climate and Weather

Define It!

atmosphere: layers of air that circle Earth

climate: weather over a long period

desert: a dry climate with little rainfall

tropical: a climate where it rains almost every day and stays warm all year-round

weather: what happens in the atmosphere

How are **climate** and **weather** different? Weather is what is happening now in the **atmosphere** in a certain place. Climate is the weather over a long period of time in a certain place. One day the weather might be cloudy or rainy in a city, but that city could have a dry, **desert** climate. Or the weather could be sunny and dry one day in a city that has a wet, **tropical** climate. Unlike the weather, which may change from one day to the next, climate does not change quickly. Changes in climate happen slowly over hundreds, thousands, and even millions of years.

desert

tropical

Complete the sentences.

1. Two kinds of climate are _____.

2. Weather can change quickly, but climate change happens

_____.

Concept:

The gases in the atmosphere trap the energy of the sun and keep Earth warm.

Earth Is a Greenhouse

What is a **greenhouse** like on a cool winter's day? It's warm enough inside to grow plants, because a greenhouse is made of glass. The rays of the sun warm the inside, and the glass keeps the warmth in. Earth is like a greenhouse. The **gases** of the atmosphere trap the sun's warmth and keep Earth warm. These gases are sometimes called *greenhouse gases*. Scientists say that Earth's greenhouse is warming up too quickly because people are putting more greenhouse gases into the atmosphere. **Carbon dioxide** is a greenhouse gas that comes from burning **fuels**. When people use fuels for things such as running more cars and heating more buildings, then more carbon dioxide goes into the atmosphere. Scientists think that the extra gases are causing Earth's climate to change.

Circle *true* or *false*.

1. Carbon dioxide is a gas in the atmosphere.   **true**   **false**

2. Burning fuels makes carbon dioxide.   **true**   **false**

3. Earth's greenhouse is cooling quickly.   **true**   **false**

Coral Reefs in Trouble

A **coral reef** is a rocky form made from the hard parts of tiny animals called *corals*. Some reefs can stretch for hundreds of miles or kilometers in warm, shallow ocean waters. Octopuses, sea stars, sea turtles, and many kinds of fish are at home in the **ecosystem** of a coral reef. Scientists have noticed that some coral reefs are not healthy. The reefs are losing their beautiful pinks, oranges, purples, and other colors. This is called **bleaching**. It happens when the ocean becomes too warm for the **algae** that live inside the corals. Without the algae, the corals bleach and die. Scientists think that extra greenhouse gases are causing the oceans to warm up, and this harms the coral reefs.

Answer the questions.

1. What things live in a coral reef ecosystem? _____

_____

2. What is coral bleaching?

_____

climate

Kinds of Climates

Earth has many different kinds of climates, and scientists have given them different names. The pictures below show four kinds of climates. Read about each kind.

desert A dry climate with very little rain. Clear skies with no clouds make days hot and nights cold.	**tropical** It is hot and wet all year-round. Rainforests grow in this climate.
highland The climate changes as you climb the mountain. It can be hot and wet at the bottom and cold and dry at the top.	**tundra** A dry climate with cold all year-round. No trees can grow in the ground that is always frozen.

Write the name of the climate below each picture.

_____

_____

_____

_____

Climate Crossword Puzzle

Skill:

Apply content vocabulary.

Use the vocabulary words to complete the crossword puzzle.

greenhouse	tropical	desert	bleach
carbon dioxide	ecosystem	coral reef	climate

Across

2. weather over a long period of time

3. a warm climate where it rains almost every day

4. a gas found in the atmosphere

6. a glass building warmed by the sun

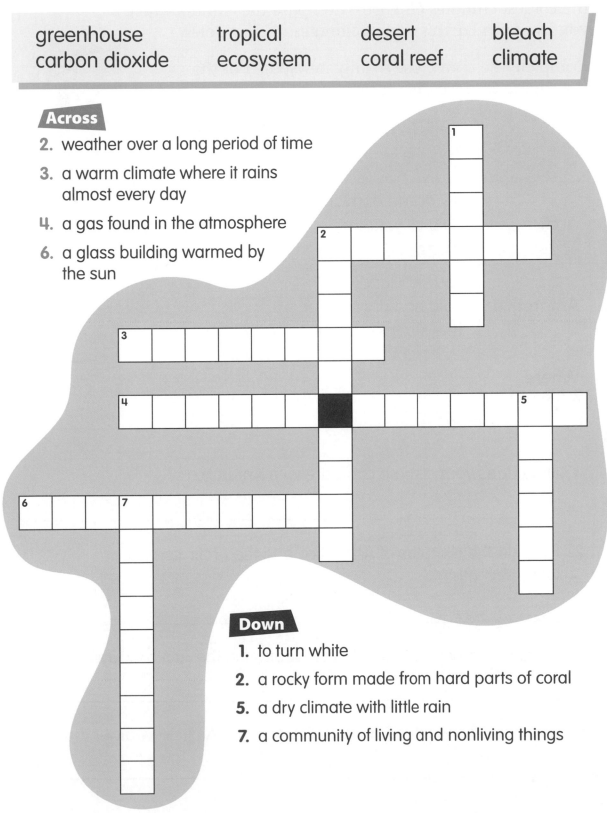

Down

1. to turn white

2. a rocky form made from hard parts of coral

5. a dry climate with little rain

7. a community of living and nonliving things

climate

Comparing Climates

Skills:

Conduct research on a science topic.

Complete a table with climate and weather information.

The Arctic (North Pole) and Antarctica (South Pole) are the coldest climates on Earth. Compare the climate where you live with Earth's coldest climates, the icy poles.

Complete the chart. Use a daily newspaper or the Internet to find weather information.

Climates and Weather

Place	What Is the Climate Like?	What Is the Weather Today?
Arctic	icy ocean and land; cold all year; stormy	
Antarctica	icy, high land; cold and dry all year; few storms reach it	
Where I Live		

1. How does your climate compare with Antarctica's?

   _____

2. How do the climates of Antarctica and the Arctic compare with each other?

   _____

3. Compare your weather with the weather in the Arctic today.

   _____

4. Compare the weather in Antarctica with the Arctic's weather today.

   _____

Earth Science: Earth and Sky   Skill Sharpeners—Science • EMC 5323 • © Evan-Moor Corp.

climate

Climate Postcard

Skills:

Follow a sequence of directions to complete a project on a science topic.

Draw and write to demonstrate knowledge of a science topic.

What You Need

- 5" x 7" (13 x 18 cm) piece of heavy paper or card stock

- ruler

- pencil

- crayons or markers

What You Do

1. Make a postcard about the climate where you live. Design the front of your postcard. Show the climate and something that people like to do in your climate. (For example, ski, swim, surf, or play baseball.)

2. Draw lines on the back of the postcard as shown.

3. Write a message that tells about the climate and gives reasons why someone should visit the place where you live.

4. Ask an adult family member for a stamp so you can mail your postcard to someone.

Having a wonderful climate. Wish you were here!

Skill:

Write an opinion about a topic, and give reasons to support a point of view.

A Climate Wish

Which climate would you like to visit someday? Give your reasons why. Include things you know about the climate.

Hint

Kinds of climates you have learned about: desert, icy poles, tundra, tropical, highland.

_____

_____

_____

_____

_____

_____

Earth Science: Earth and Sky   Skill Sharpeners—Science • EMC 5323 • © Evan-Moor Corp.

What Is a Hurricane?

Define It!

hurricane: a powerful storm with strong winds and heavy rain

storm surge: rising of the sea

swirl: to spin or whirl

tropical: areas of the Earth that are warm and close to the equator

Concepts:

A hurricane is a natural hazard that results from natural processes.

Hurricanes have powerful winds.

Floods often accompany a hurricane.

Hurricanes are the largest storms on Earth, and they cause the most damage. Hurricanes form in **tropical** areas over warm ocean waters. Often, hurricanes form over the Atlantic Ocean and travel from the west coast of Africa to the east coast of the United States. The storm grows larger as thunderstorm clouds gather in a circle pattern. Storm winds **swirl** around a center. The center of the storm is called the *eye* of the hurricane.

When hurricanes pass over land, their powerful winds can destroy buildings and tear up trees. A hurricane has winds measuring 74 miles (119 km) per hour and higher. A **storm surge**, or rise of ocean water carried by the hurricane, causes flooding.

Complete the sentences.

1. Hurricanes form in tropical areas because they need

   _____.

2. Hurricane winds destroy buildings, and a storm surge causes

   _____.

Hurricanes

Concepts:

A hurricane is a natural hazard that humans cannot eliminate, but people can take steps to reduce a hurricane's impact.

Meteorologists warn people who are in the path of a hurricane.

Hurricane Hunters

Define It!

announce: to make known

meteorologist: a weather expert

radar: a tool that uses radio waves to measure the speed of something

satellite: an object sent into space on a rocket to orbit the Earth

Hurricanes can be more than 100 miles (161 km) across and they can travel a long distance. **Meteorologists** (weather scientists) track hurricanes in order to warn people who are in a hurricane's path. Meteorologists use tools such as **radar** and **satellite** pictures from space to see where the hurricane is and in what direction it is going. Special airplanes called *hurricane hunters* gather weather data. These planes sometimes even fly into the eye of a hurricane. The National Weather Service **announces** a *hurricane watch* if there is a good chance of a hurricane forming within 48 hours. A *hurricane warning* means a hurricane is on its way within the next 36 hours, and people should leave that area or find a safe place.

Circle *true* or *false*.

1. Hurricane hunters can stop hurricanes.   **true**   **false**

2. Satellites help scientists see the path of a hurricane.   **true**   **false**

Hurricane Plans

Concepts:

A hurricane is a natural hazard that humans cannot eliminate, but people can take steps to reduce a hurricane's impact.

Engineers study hurricane damage in order to create stronger buildings.

People cannot stop hurricanes, but they can plan ahead to help save lives and **property**. Hurricane Andrew struck the United States in August 1992. It was one of the worst storms in U.S. history. The winds were stronger than 160 miles (257 km) per hour. Andrew destroyed almost the entire city of Homestead, Florida.

After Andrew, **engineers** looked at the **damage** done to buildings. Roofs that had been built with thin wood and staples blew off. The engineers wanted new rules for building houses. Today, houses must be built with a new kind of stronger roof nail. The wood has to be stronger, too. New homes must also have storm **shutters** that cover windows, or special window glass that will hold up if something hits it. Hospitals now have heavy metal doors with rubber seals to keep out the waters of a storm surge.

Answer the questions.

1. Where did hurricane Andrew cause a lot of damage?

_____

2. How do engineers want roofs to be built?

_____

Skills:

Label a graphic image to show the working parts of something in nature.

Analyze and interpret information presented in both a text and a photo.

A Look from Space

The first weather satellite was launched into space in 1960. Today's satellites give meteorologists a good look at hurricanes from space. Satellite pictures taken over time show how fast a hurricane is growing and the path it is taking.

Read the hurricane words and information below. Then label the satellite picture.

Eye The eye is the center of the storm. The eye has calm winds and clear skies. It can be 20 to 40 miles (32 to 64 km) across.

Eye Wall The eye wall is a thick wall of thunderclouds around the eye. The eye wall has the strongest winds and the most rain.

Rain Bands These thick bands of thunderclouds spin around the eye in a pinwheel shape.

Counterclockwise Direction Thunderclouds spin in the opposite direction of the hands on a clock.

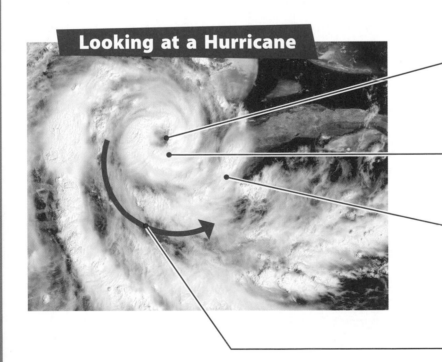

Looking at a Hurricane

Earth Science: Earth and Sky

Hurricanes Crossword Puzzle

Use the vocabulary words to complete the crossword puzzle.

hurricane	announce	satellite	tropical
meteorologist	engineer	property	radar

Across

2. a weather expert

5. something that is owned

7. to make known

8. a tool that uses radio waves to measure the speed of something

Down

1. areas of the Earth that are warm and near the equator

3. a person who uses science to plan buildings and other things

4. an object sent into space on a rocket to orbit the Earth

6. a powerful storm with strong winds and heavy rain

Being Ready

Skills:

Write and reflect for the purpose of planning.

Demonstrate knowledge of hurricane readiness.

It is important for people who live in a hurricane area to have a plan and be ready to leave. They may have to be gone for a few days. It is a good idea to make a list ahead of time of things they will need to take.

If you lived in a hurricane area and needed to leave with your family, what would you take with you? Think about the important things you would need in each group below. Make a list.

For Sleeping

_____

_____

_____

Books, Games, Music

_____

_____

_____

For Keeping Clean

_____

_____

_____

Medicine and First Aid

_____

_____

_____

Food/Snacks and Drinks

_____

_____

_____

Other Things

_____

_____

_____

Hurricanes

Plan for a Hurricane

People who live in a hurricane area should have a plan. Make a poster to remind people to be ready for a hurricane. Design your poster with the hurricane flags that are used to warn ships and the hurricane symbols used on maps and signs.

What You Need

- pencil and paper
- poster board (a light color)
- construction paper (red, black)
- crayons or markers
- scissors
- glue

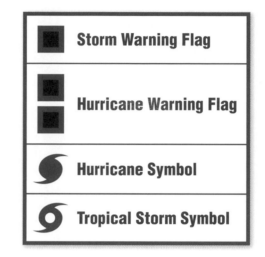

■	**Storm Warning Flag**
■ ■	**Hurricane Warning Flag**
🌀	**Hurricane Symbol**
🌀	**Tropical Storm Symbol**

What You Do

1. Plan your poster. Draw it with paper and pencil first. Think of a short saying that people will remember, for example, "Be Ready!"

2. Draw and cut out hurricane flags and symbols from construction paper.

3. Write the saying on your poster.

4. Glue on the flags and symbols.

5. Hang your poster.

Skills:

Follow a sequence of directions to complete a science project.

Acquire awareness of hurricane symbols used in warnings.

Hurricanes

Earth Science: Earth and Sky

About a Hurricane

Have you been in a hurricane? Write about what happened. If you have not been in a hurricane, write about one that you have heard or read about in the news. Give the name of the hurricane and tell what you know about it.

_____

_____

_____

_____

_____

_____

_____

Tornado!

Tornadoes are some of the strongest storms on Earth. A tornado is a fast-spinning **column** of air, called a **vortex**. It stretches from a thundercloud to the ground. Tornado winds can sometimes spin at 300 miles (483 km) per hour. We are able to see tornado winds because they contain water, dust, and pieces of objects they have picked up. A tornado is powerful enough to lift cars and even houses. The **swirling** winds of a tornado can smash everything in its path. Tornadoes happen in many parts of the world, but most of them **occur** in the United States. About 1,200 tornadoes are reported in the U.S. each year.

Define It!

column: a tall, straight post

occur: to happen

swirl: to spin or whirl

vortex: a mass of whirling air

Concepts:

A tornado is a natural hazard that results from natural processes.

Tornadoes have powerful, swirling winds.

Circle *true* or *false.*

1. Tornadoes occur only in the United States.   true   false

2. A tornado is a vortex.   true   false

3. A tornado is one of Earth's most powerful storms.   true   false

Concepts:

Tornadoes are natural hazards that people cannot eliminate, however, people can take steps to reduce a tornado's impact.

Scientists study tornadoes to understand them better and to be able to forecast them more accurately.

Tornadoes

Tornado Forecast

Define It!

forecast: to tell what will happen ahead of time

model: a small copy

radar: a tool that measures speed

satellite: an object sent into space to orbit Earth

weather balloon: a balloon with tools to measure weather

Scientists would like to learn more about tornadoes. They want to be better able to **forecast** these killer storms so they can warn people sooner. Tornadoes happen most often during the spring and summer, when powerful thunderstorms occur. But they can happen any time of year. Scientists do not know exactly how tornadoes form.

Because tornadoes move quickly, it is difficult for scientists to study them. Scientists use data from **satellites** and **weather balloons** to forecast bad weather that may produce tornadoes. They also use **radar** to look for spinning patterns that could form tornadoes. Scientists are able to use math to make computer **models** of a tornado, and then study how it changes.

Complete the sentences.

1. A computer _____ can help scientists study tornadoes.

2. Scientists want to _____ a tornado to help save lives.

3. Radar shows weather _____ that could become a tornado.

Tornado Safety

Define It!

drill: to learn by doing something again and again

siren: an object that makes a loud warning sound

storm shelter: an underground room made to protect people in a tornado

Concepts:

People learn and practice safety procedures to protect themselves from a natural hazard.

Watches, warnings, and drills help people reduce the impact of a natural hazard.

When tornado weather patterns are spotted, the National Weather Service announces a *tornado watch*. This means that people in the area should pay close attention to the sky. They should watch or listen to the TV, the Internet, or a radio for warnings. If a *tornado warning* is given, a tornado has been seen on radar or spotted by someone. It means that people should quickly take cover in a safe place. Some communities sound special **sirens** as a warning.

People need to know ahead of time what to do if a tornado is coming. Tornado **drills** give them practice in where to go and what to do. The safest place to be is underground in a basement or a **storm shelter**. If one of these is not nearby, then go to a small inside room or hallway without windows. People who are outside or in a car should look for a ditch and lie down in it.

Answer the questions.

1. When is a tornado warning given? _____

_____

2. Why are tornado drills important? _____

_____

Tornadoes

Skills:

Analyze and interpret information presented in a table.

Develop a list using information presented in a table.

Tornado Count

Since 1950, scientists have kept records of the number of tornadoes in the United States. The total count for 2011 was 1,691. The table below shows how many tornadoes occurred in each month of 2011.

Look at the table and answer the questions.

Number of Tornadoes in 2011	
January	16
February	63
March	75
April	758
May	326
June	160
July	103
August	57
September	51
October	23
November	44
December	15

1. Which month of 2011 had the most tornadoes? _____

2. Which month had the fewest tornadoes? _____

3. List the top five tornado months of 2011 in order, starting with the month that had the most.

   _____

   _____

   _____

   _____

Earth Science: Earth and Sky   *Skill Sharpeners—Science • EMC 5323 • © Evan-Moor Corp.*

Tornadoes

Either/Or Questions

Write each answer.

1. Is a column like a balloon **or** a post? _____

2. Is a siren a wind **or** a warning? _____

3. In a drill, do you spin **or** practice? _____

4. Is a weather balloon used to forecast **or** to play? _____

5. Can radar spot a storm shelter **or** a tornado? _____

6. Is a storm shelter a safe place **or** a model? _____

7. Is a satellite in space **or** underground? _____

8. Does a vortex forecast **or** swirl? _____

Tornadoes

Tornado in a Bottle

Skills:

Conduct a demonstration to illustrate a concept from the lesson.

Make observations and describe what was observed.

A tornado is a vortex of swirling winds that forms when a storm causes air to rise very quickly. You can create a model of a swirling vortex with water and two plastic bottles.

What You Need

- 2 clear plastic bottles, empty
- waterproof tape, such as duct tape
- water

What You Do

1. Make sure the bottles are clean, and peel off any labels.

2. Fill one of the bottles two-thirds full with water.

3. Cover the mouth of the empty bottle with tape. Ask an adult to help poke a hole in it. Holes of different sizes will create "tornadoes" with different features.

4. Use tape to fasten the bottles together at the mouth, with the empty one on top. Use enough tape so that no water will leak out. Turn the bottles over so that the water is on top. Immediately swirl the bottles. Look for the vortex inside the top bottle.

What Did You Discover?

What happens to the water as it flows from the top bottle into the bottom bottle?

_____

_____

Tornadoes

Swirling String Tornadoes

Skills:

Follow a sequence of directions to complete a science project.

Interpret nature with art.

What You Need

- 12" (30 cm) piece of thin yarn or string
- black tempera paint
- shallow dish
- sheet of white drawing paper
- piece of cardboard about the same size as half a sheet of drawing paper
- newspaper

What You Do

1. Spread newspaper on your work surface. Fold the sheet of drawing paper in half and then open it.

2. Pour a small amount of paint into the dish. Dip the yarn into the paint. Leave about 1" (2.5 cm) at one end without paint. Use your fingers to evenly coat the yarn.

3. Place the yarn on one half of the paper in an interesting shape. Leave the unpainted end off the paper. Clean the paint off your fingers.

4. Fold the other half of the paper over the yarn. Leave the end of the yarn sticking out. Place the cardboard on top.

5. Hold the cardboard down flat with one hand and pull the string out with the other hand. Pull it in different directions.

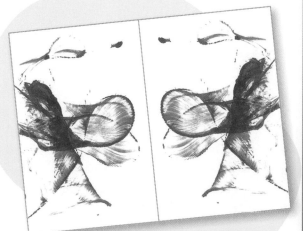

6. Open the paper to see a vortex. Dip the yarn in the paint again, place the string, and repeat.

Earth Science: Earth and Sky

Skill:

Write and draw a sequence of steps that can be taken in order to stay safe from a natural hazard.

Tornado Tip

Help others learn about tornado safety. Draw and write a cartoon about a safety tip. Make up a character and use the boxes to show how the character stays safe.

Tornado Safety Tips!

Have tornado drills to practice what to do.
A tornado warning means take cover quickly.
Go to a basement or a storm shelter underground.

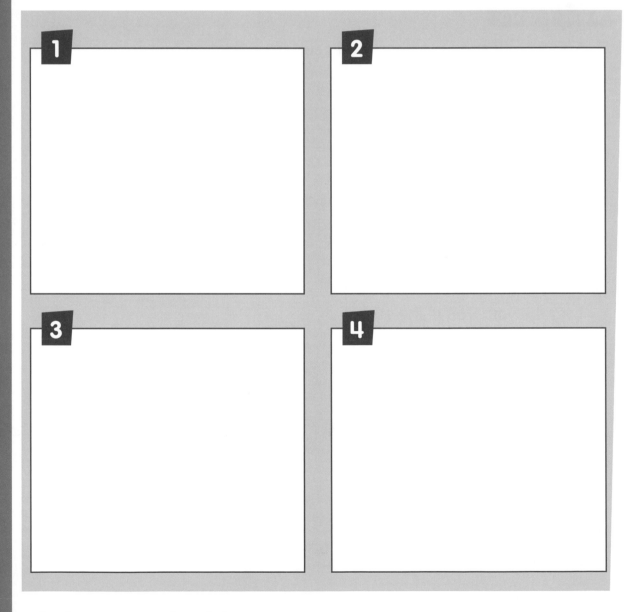

1

2

3

4

Tornadoes

Earth Science: Earth and Sky Skill Sharpeners—Science • EMC 5323 • © Evan-Moor Corp.

About Floods

When a body of water covers an area that is usually dry land, that is a flood. Areas near rivers, lakes, and oceans can flood. River floods are the most common. Many rivers have a **cycle** of dry times and flooding. Rivers and lakes may flow over their **banks** when there is more rain than usual, or when snow and ice melt suddenly. Hurricanes can bring floods to areas along ocean coasts.

Although it can sometimes do good things, such as bring new soil to an area, a flood is a **natural hazard**. Farms and crops may be destroyed by a flood. In an area where many people live, floods can be a danger to people's lives. More lives are lost in floods than in any other kind of weather. Floods destroy **property**, and building over again after a flood can cost billions of dollars.

Define It!

banks: land at the edge of a river

cycle: a pattern of events that happen in the same order

natural hazard: an event in nature that causes harm to people and property

property: something that is owned

Concepts:

Floods are a natural hazard that results from natural processes.

A flood can cause harm to people and property.

sittitap / Shutterstock.com

Answer the questions.

1. What can happen to rivers when snow and ice suddenly melt?

_____

2. What can happen to crops in a flood?

_____

Ancient Floods

Define It!

ancient: belonging to times long past

control: to hold back

dam: a barrier to hold back water

nutrients: elements in soil that are needed by plants

silt: fine sand or clay carried by water

The Nile River in Africa is the longest river in the world. In **ancient** times in Egypt, the Nile River flooded every year. To the people of ancient Egypt, the flooding Nile was a force of good. The river carried **silt**, or rich new soil. When the floodwaters went away, the rich soil remained. The new soil contained **nutrients** that were good for growing crops. The Nile was so important to the ancient people that their calendar was based on its cycle. The new year began in the middle of summer, when the river began to rise. Today, there is a huge **dam** on the Nile at Aswan, Egypt. The dam was completed in 1970. It **controls** floods in the rainy season and stores water to be used later.

Circle *true* or *false*.

1. The Nile River floods carried away old soil.   **true**   **false**

2. The people of ancient Egypt built a dam on the Nile.   **true**   **false**

3. The Nile is the world's longest river.   **true**   **false**

Floods

Flood Control

Engineers plan dams that are built to control flooding. Hoover Dam stands on the Colorado River between Arizona and Nevada. Before Hoover Dam was built, melting snow in the mountains caused the Colorado River to flood every spring. Floods destroyed thousands of **acres** of crops. But by summer, the river didn't hold enough water for farms. Hoover Dam was built to control the Colorado River. Behind the dam is a giant **reservoir** of water called Lake Mead. The water in the reservoir is used by farmers in Nevada, Arizona, and California to water crops. The water also goes to cities in southern California. Engineers control the water falling through the dam, and this water moves **turbines** that make **electric** power. The power is used in California, Nevada, and Arizona.

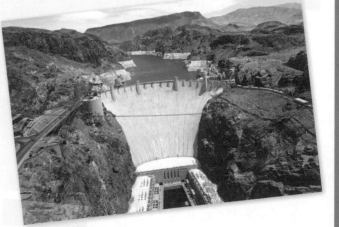

Complete the sentences.

1. Hoover Dam controls floods on the _____ .

2. Lake Mead is a _____ of water used by farms and cities.

3. Hoover Dam produces _____ .

Floods

Skills:

Analyze and interpret information presented in text and illustrations.

Label photos that illustrate a variety of types of structures.

Types of Dams

Engineers build dams in different shapes and with different materials. Some dams are made from earth and others from concrete. Concrete is sand, stones, cement, and water mixed together. Concrete hardens and becomes very strong.

Read about each type of dam. Then label the pictures to tell which type of dam each one is.

Embankment Dam

An embankment is a wall or bank of earth. The Fort Peck Dam in Montana is an embankment dam.

Gravity Dam It is thick and made of concrete. Its huge weight holds back the water. The Grand Coulee Dam in Washington state is a gravity dam.

Buttress Dam Tall supports called *buttresses* hold up the dam. The Bartlett Dam in Arizona is a buttress dam.

Arch Dam It has a curved shape and is often built between two walls of rock. The Glen Canyon Dam in Arizona is an arch dam.

1. Glen Canyon Dam

_____

2. Bartlett Dam

_____

3. Grand Coulee Dam

_____

4. Fort Peck Dam

_____

Earth Science: Earth and Sky

Skill Sharpeners—Science • EMC 5323 • © Evan-Moor Corp.

Floods Crossword Puzzle

Skill:

Apply content vocabulary.

Use the vocabulary words to complete the crossword puzzle.

banks	engineer	cycle	dam
ancient	reservoir	silt	turbine

Across

3. a machine for making power with a wheel turned by water
4. fine sand or clay carried by water
5. a person who plans things to be built
8. belonging to times long past

Down

1. a pattern of events that happen in the same order
2. a large lake used as a water supply
6. land at the edge of a river
7. a barrier to hold back water

Floods

Make a Working Waterwheel

A waterwheel is a machine that changes the energy of falling water into power. The power of the waterwheel turns an axle, or rod. A dam uses the power of falling water to run a motor that makes electricity. You can make a waterwheel with power to lift a weight.

What You Need

- 2 or more sturdy paper plates
- scissors
- pencil
- 12" (30 cm) piece of yarn
- large paper clip
- sink with running water

What You Do

1. Ask an adult to poke a tiny hole in the center of a paper plate, using scissors.

2. Poke the pencil halfway through the hole so the pencil fits snugly.

3. Cut slits about 2" (5 cm) apart around the edge of another plate. Bend them back and cut them off for flaps. Cut a small slit at the bottom of each flap as shown.

Earth Science: Earth and Sky

Skill Sharpeners—Science • EMC 5323 • © Evan-Moor Corp.

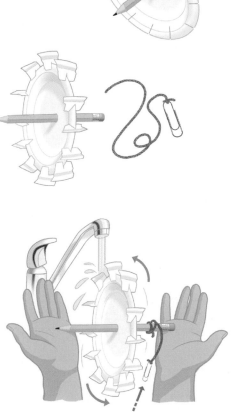

4. Cut ½" (1.3 cm) slits into the edge of the first paper plate, about 2" (5 cm) apart. Fit a flap into each slit on the paper plate, slits together as shown.

5. Tie the paper clip to one end of the yarn. Decide where on the pencil to tie the other end of the yarn. Then test your idea.

6. Lay the ends of the pencil on your open hands with palms up, so both the waterwheel and the pencil can turn. Let the yarn and the paper clip drop down from the pencil. Hold the waterwheel over the sink in a stream of water as shown.

7. The wheel will turn, causing the pencil to spin. The yarn should wind around the pencil, lifting the paper clip.

What Did You Discover?

Did your idea work?

_____

What happens when you slide the yarn to a different place on the pencil? Explain.

_____

_____

Can you make the yarn unwind and lower the paper clip? How?

_____

_____

Floods

Thinking About Floods

There is more than one way to think about floods. Floods are a natural hazard, but the people of ancient Egypt considered them to be a good thing.

Write some ideas to support each way of thinking.

1. Floods are a natural hazard.

_____

_____

_____

2. In ancient Egypt, floods were helpful.

_____

_____

_____

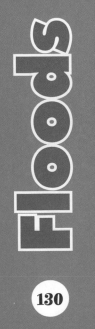

Answer Key

Page 3

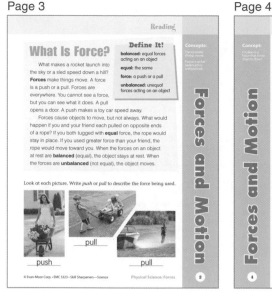

What Is Force?

What makes a rocket launch into the sky or a sled speed down a hill? **Forces** make things move. A force is a push or a pull. Forces are everywhere. You cannot see a force, but you can see what it does. A pull opens a door. A push makes a toy car speed away.

Forces cause objects to move, but not always. What would happen if you and your friend each pulled on opposite ends of a rope? If you both tugged with **equal** force, the rope would stay in place. If you used greater force than your friend, the rope would move toward you. When the forces on an object at rest are **balanced** (equal), the object stays at rest. When the forces are **unbalanced** (not equal), the object moves.

Define It!
balanced: equal forces acting on an object
equal: the same
force: a push or a pull
unbalanced: unequal forces acting on an object

Look at each picture. Write *push* or *pull* to describe the force being used.

pull

push   pull

Page 4

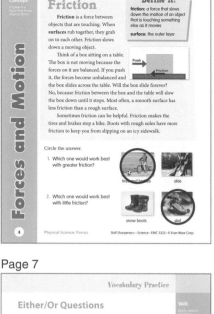

Friction

Friction is a force between objects that are touching. When **surfaces** rub together, they grab onto each other. Friction slows down a moving object.

Think of a box sitting on a table. The box is not moving because the forces on it are balanced. If you push it, the forces become unbalanced and the box slides across the table. Will the box slide forever? No, because friction between the box and the table will slow the box down until it stops. Most often, a smooth surface has less friction than a rough surface.

Sometimes friction can be helpful. Friction makes the tires and brakes stop a bike. Boots with rough soles have more friction to keep you from slipping on an icy sidewalk.

Define It!
friction: a force that slows down the motion of an object that is touching something else as it moves
surface: the outer layer

Circle the answer.

1. Which one would work best with greater friction?
   tires and brakes   slide

2. Which one would work best with little friction?
   snow boots   sled

Page 5

Force and Motion

Forces change the **motion** of objects. Forces make objects speed up and slow down. Forces make objects change direction and change shape.

speed up   slow down   change direction   change shape

A force has both **size** and **direction**. Think about a soccer ball. What happens when you try to make a goal? To get the ball into the goal, you kick it with the right amount (size) of force. If you use too little force, the ball will not reach the goal. You also aim (direct) the force so that the ball goes into the net. If the direction of the force is off, the ball will miss the goal.

Define It!
direction: the line along which something travels
motion: the act of moving
size: the amount of something

Draw a line under the answer.

1. Squeezing a tube of toothpaste shows that force can ____.
   slow things down   **change the shape of things**

2. Batting a baseball shows that force changes the ____ of an object.
   direction   size

Page 6

Picturing Forces

Forces cannot be seen, but we can see what they do. Forces change the motion of objects. In order to show how forces work, scientists make drawings. Arrows in the drawings show the direction of the forces. Arrows also show the size of the forces. A longer arrow stands for a stronger force.

Push   Pull   Friction
toward the object   away from the object

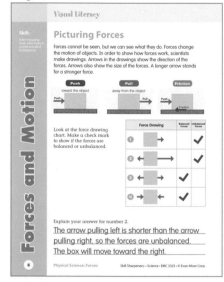

Look at the force drawing chart. Make a check mark to show if the forces are balanced or unbalanced.

Force Drawing	Balanced Forces	Unbalanced Forces
1		✓
2		✓
3	✓	
4		✓

Explain your answer for number 2.
The arrow pulling left is shorter than the arrow pulling right, so the forces are unbalanced. The box will move toward the right.

Page 7

Either/Or Questions

Write each answer.

1. Is a push a size **or** a force?   a force
2. Is a pull a force **or** a surface?   a force
3. If forces are balanced, are they equal **or** unequal?   equal
4. Does friction slow things down **or** speed things up?   slow things down
5. If an object moves, is it at rest **or** in motion?   in motion
6. Is the surface of a slide smooth **or** rough?   smooth
7. Does the direction of a force control how far an object goes **or** where an object goes?   where an object goes
8. Are unbalanced forces equal **or** unequal?   unequal
9. Does the size of a force change the speed of an object **or** the direction of an object?   speed
10. Is a force seen **or** unseen?   unseen

Think About It
Is a force real or unreal? How do you know?
You cannot see a force, but it is real because you can see what it does.

Page 8

Marshmallow Popper

How can you make a marshmallow fly? This activity shows how the size of a force changes the distance an object travels.

What You Need
• yogurt cup   • mini marshmallows
• scissors   • sidewalk chalk
• balloon

What You Do

1. Ask an adult to cut out the bottom of a yogurt cup.
2. Tie a knot at the open end of the balloon and cut off about ½" (1.3 cm) from the other end.
3. Stretch the cut end of the balloon over the top rim of the yogurt cup.
4. Go outside on a paved surface if possible. Drop a mini marshmallow into the cup, pull back on the knotted end of the balloon, aim into the distance, and let go.
5. How far did the marshmallow travel? Mark the place where it landed with sidewalk chalk. How can you make the distance longer or shorter? Test your idea. Mark each landing place.
6. Pulling back on the balloon and then letting go creates a force that pushes the marshmallow.

How did you make the force greater?
by pulling on the balloon more

How did the size of a force change the distance traveled by the marshmallow?
The greater the force, the farther the marshmallow traveled.

Page 10

Show What You Know

Look at the picture. List two examples of each force at work.

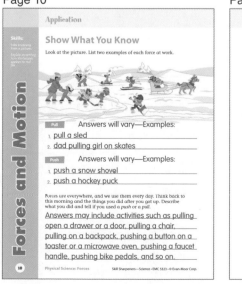

Pull   Answers will vary—Examples:
1. pull a sled
2. dad pulling girl on skates

Push   Answers will vary—Examples:
1. push a snow shovel
2. push a hockey puck

Forces are everywhere, and we use them every day. Think back to this morning and the things you did after you got up. Describe what you did and tell if you used a *push* or a *pull*.
Answers may include activities such as pulling open a drawer or a door, pulling a chair, pulling on a backpack, pushing a button on a toaster or a microwave oven, pushing a faucet handle, pushing bike pedals, and so on.

Page 11

Magnets Attract Metals

What makes the notes stick on this refrigerator door? Not glue, but an unseen force called **magnetism**! Magnetism is the force that makes **magnets** pull, or **attract**, some kinds of metal. The metal refrigerator door is attracted to magnets. A magnet will not attract glass, plastic, wood, or anything else that does not contain metal.

Magnets stick to objects made of metal, but not all metals. The metal **iron**, or a metal that has iron in it, is attracted to a magnet. A magnet won't stick to coins or soda cans. They are not made of iron.

Define It!
attract: to pull
iron: a blue-gray metal that can be made into a magnet
magnet: an object that attracts iron
magnetism: the force that attracts iron

1. Draw an X on the objects that will **not** be attracted to a magnet.

2. Which objects above may have iron in them? How could you test them?
The paper clip and the pin may have iron in them. I'd test them by seeing if they stick to a magnet.

Page 12

Magnets Push and Pull

All magnets have a **magnetic field** that you cannot see. It's the area around the magnet where a force pulls objects toward the magnet. Magnets have two **poles**. The poles are the parts of the magnet where its force is the strongest. Every magnet has a north pole and a south pole. N stands for *north* and S stands for *south*.

When two magnets are held with their north and south poles together, the poles attract each other. They pull together. But two poles of the same kind repel one another. They push away.

Define It!
magnetic field: the space around a magnet where its force can be found
pole: either end of a magnet
repel: to push away

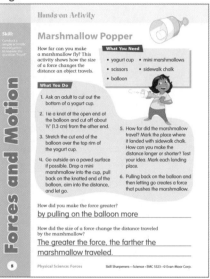

A   B

1. Which picture shows magnets that will attract?   A **B**
2. Which picture shows magnets that will repel?   **A** B

Page 13

Magnets: Strong or Weak?

Define It!
magnetic: able to attract iron or act like a magnet
strength: power
weak: lacking strength

Which magnets are stronger—big ones or small ones? You cannot know the strength of a magnet just by its size. The **strength** of a magnet has to do with its magnetic field. A strong **magnetic** field will attract more than a **weak** magnetic field will. The stronger magnetic field will attract things that are farther away or that are heavier.

Look at these two magnets. You cannot see the magnetic force around a magnet. But the lines in these pictures show where the magnetic fields are. The field shown with more lines is stronger. Trace the magnetic fields.

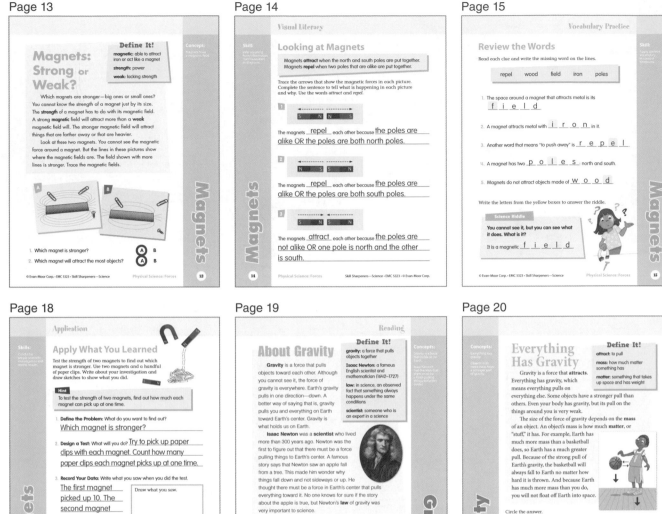

1. Which magnet is stronger? **A** B
2. Which magnet will attract the most objects? **A** B

Page 14

Looking at Magnets

Magnets **attract** when the north and south poles are put together. Magnets **repel** when two poles that are alike are put together.

Trace the arrows that show the magnetic forces in each picture. Complete the sentence to tell what is happening in each picture and why. Use the words *attract* and *repel*.

1. The magnets _repel_ each other because the poles are alike OR the poles are both north poles.

2. The magnets _repel_ each other because the poles are alike OR the poles are both south poles.

3. The magnets _attract_ each other because the poles are not alike OR one pole is north and the other is south.

Page 15

Review the Words

Read each clue and write the missing word on the lines.

repel   wood   field   iron   poles

1. The space around a magnet that attracts metal is its
   f i e l d

2. A magnet attracts metal with i r o n in it.

3. Another word that means "to push away" is r e p e l

4. A magnet has two p o l e s : north and south.

5. Magnets do not attract objects made of w o o d

Write the letters from the yellow boxes to answer the riddle.

Science Riddle
You cannot see it, but you can see what it does. What is it?
It is a magnetic f i e l d

Page 18

Apply What You Learned

Test the strength of two magnets to find out which magnet is stronger. Use two magnets and a handful of paper clips. Write about your investigation and draw sketches to show what you did.

Hint
To test the strength of two magnets, find out how much each magnet can pick up at one time.

1. **Define the Problem:** What do you want to find out?
   Which magnet is stronger?

2. **Design a Test:** What will you do? Try to pick up paper clips with each magnet. Count how many paper clips each magnet picks up at one time.

3. **Record Your Data:** Write what you saw when you did the test.
   The first magnet picked up 10. The second magnet picked up 7.
   [Draw what you saw.]

4. **Write About the Results:** What did you find out?
   The first magnet is stronger.

Page 19

About Gravity

Define It!
gravity: a force that pulls objects together
Isaac Newton: a famous English scientist and mathematician (1642–1727)
law: in science, an observed fact that something always happens under the same conditions
scientist: someone who is an expert in a science

Gravity is a force that pulls objects toward each other. Although you cannot see it, the force of gravity is everywhere. Earth's gravity pulls in one direction—down. A better way of saying that is, gravity pulls you and everything on Earth toward Earth's center. Gravity is what holds us on Earth.

Isaac Newton was a **scientist** who lived more than 300 years ago. Newton was the first to figure out that there must be a force pulling things to Earth's center. A famous story says that Newton saw an apple fall from a tree. This made him wonder why things fall down and not sideways or up. He thought there must be a force in Earth's center that pulls everything toward it. No one knows for sure if the story about the apple is true, but Newton's **law** of gravity was very important to science.

Complete the sentences.

1. An apple falls down from a tree, instead of up, because
   the force of gravity pulls it down

2. _Isaac Newton_ thought about why objects fall to Earth.

Page 20

Everything Has Gravity

Define It!
attract: to pull
mass: how much matter something has
matter: something that takes up space and has weight

Gravity is a force that **attracts**. Everything has gravity, which means everything pulls on everything else. Some objects have a stronger pull than others. Even your body has gravity, but its pull on the things around you is very weak.

The size of the force of gravity depends on the **mass** of an object. An object's mass is how much **matter**, or "stuff," it has. For example, Earth has much more mass than a basketball does, so Earth has a much greater pull. Because of the strong pull of Earth's gravity, the basketball will always fall to Earth no matter how hard it is thrown. And because Earth has much more mass than you do, you will not float off Earth into space.

Circle the answer.

1. Which one has more gravity? **Earth**   (girl / Earth)
2. Which one has more mass? **Earth**   (book / Earth)

Page 21

Gravity and Weight

Define It!
astronaut: a person who travels to outer space
weight: a measure of the pull of gravity on an object
weightless: having no gravity pulling on it

To a scientist, mass and **weight** are not the same thing. Your weight is a measure of the pull of gravity on you. **Astronauts** traveling in space are **weightless** because there is no gravity pulling on them. Their weight is zero. But their mass is the same as it was on Earth.

Other planets, moons, and stars have their own gravity. So if you visited other worlds, your weight would be different from your weight on Earth. A person who weighs 60 pounds (about 27 kg) on Earth would only weigh about 23 pounds (about 10 kg) on Mars. The same person would weigh about 142 pounds (about 64 kg) on Jupiter.

Earth has a very large mass. This means that it has a strong force of gravity, too. The moon is smaller than Earth and has less gravity. Would you weigh more on the moon or less? Why?

I would weigh less on the moon. The moon has less gravity, and weight depends on how much gravity is pulling on you.

Page 22

Playground Forces

Have you ever looked at a playground to see forces in action? Let's look at what happens when Ava sits on a swing. A force is needed to set the swing in motion. The swing will move when someone pushes Ava or when she pulls back and pumps her legs. After that, forces carry Ava up and gravity pulls her down. You can predict the pattern of motion. If the swing goes forward and up, next it will go down. Then the swing will go backward and up, down again. When Ava drags her feet on the ground, she creates enough force to stop the swing. If Ava simply stopped pumping her legs, the swing would stop by itself because of the force of the air.

Number these mixed-up pictures from 1 to 5 to show the pattern of motion.

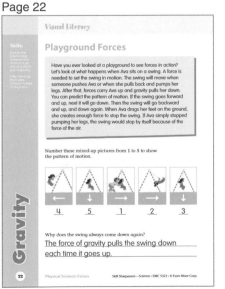

4   5   1   2   3

Why does the swing always come down again?
The force of gravity pulls the swing down each time it goes up.

Page 23

Gravity Crossword Puzzle

Use the vocabulary words to complete the crossword puzzle.

attract   weight   gravity   Newton
matter   weightless   scientist   astronaut

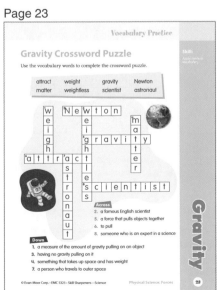

Across
2. a famous English scientist
5. a force that pulls objects together
6. to pull
8. someone who is an expert in a science

Down
1. a measure of the amount of gravity pulling on an object
3. having no gravity pulling on it
4. something that takes up space and has weight
7. a person who travels to outer space

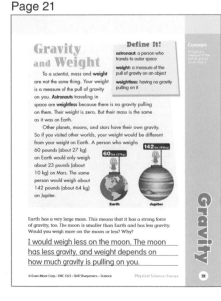

Page 24

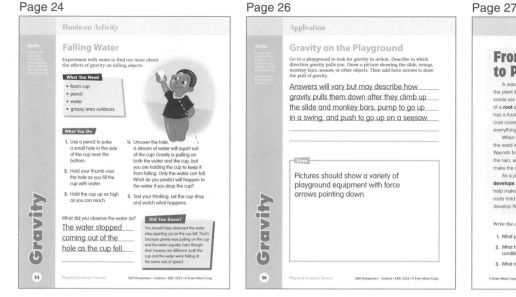

Falling Water

Experiment with water to find out more about the effects of gravity on falling objects.

What You Need
- foam cup
- pencil
- water
- grassy area outdoors

What You Do

1. Use a pencil to poke a small hole in the side of the cup near the bottom.
2. Hold your thumb over the hole as you fill the cup with water.
3. Hold the cup up as high as you can reach.
4. Uncover the hole. A stream of water will squirt out of the cup! Gravity is pulling on both the water and the cup, but you are holding the cup to keep it from falling. Only the water can fall. What do you predict will happen to the water if you drop the cup?
5. Test your thinking. Let the cup drop and watch what happens.

What did you observe the water do?
The water stopped coming out of the hole as the cup fell.

Did You Know?
You should have observed the water stop squirting out as the cup fell. That's because gravity was pulling on the cup and the water equally. Even though their masses are different, both the cup and the water were falling at the same rate of speed.

Gravity

24   Physical Science: Forces   Skill Sharpeners—Science • EMC 5323 • © Evan-Moor Corp.

Page 26

Application

Gravity on the Playground

Go to a playground to look for gravity in action. Describe in which direction gravity pulls you. Draw a picture showing the slide, swings, monkey bars, seesaw, or other objects. Then add force arrows to show the pull of gravity.

Answers will vary but may describe how gravity pulls them down after they climb up the slide and monkey bars, pump to go up in a swing, and push to go up on a seesaw.

Draw

Pictures should show a variety of playground equipment with force arrows pointing down.

Gravity

26   Physical Science: Forces   Skill Sharpeners—Science • EMC 5323 • © Evan-Moor Corp.

Page 27

Reading

From Seed to Plant

A seed doesn't look like the plant it will become. But inside are the tiny beginnings of a **root** and a stem. The seed has a food supply, too. A seed coat covers and protects everything inside the seed.

When **conditions** are right, the seed will **germinate**, or grow. Warmth from the sun, water from the rain, and food from the soil make the right conditions for growth.

As a plant grows taller, it also **develops** new parts. Its new leaves help make food for the plant. New roots hold it in the soil. Many plants develop flowers.

Define It!

conditions: the weather, soil, and light affecting growth

develop: to grow into an adult

germinate: to begin to grow; to sprout

root: a plant part that grows down into the soil

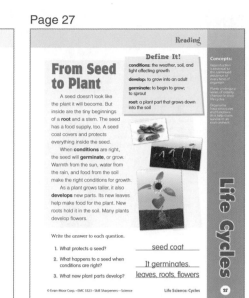

Write the answer to each question.

1. What protects a seed?   seed coat
2. What happens to a seed when conditions are right?   It germinates.
3. What new plant parts develop?   leaves, roots, flowers

Life Cycles

© Evan-Moor Corp. • EMC 5323 • Skill Sharpeners—Science   Life Science: Cycles   27

Page 28

Concepts:

Flowers and Their Seeds

Almost all plants on Earth have flowers. Flowers are beautiful to look at and they smell good, but they also do important work for the plant. Flowers make seeds, which are needed for the plant to **reproduce**, or make new plants. Sometimes the seeds drop to the ground. Other seeds are carried away and dropped by animals or by the wind. Many flowering plants produce their seeds and then die. When the conditions are right, the seeds will produce new plants. A whole new **life cycle** will begin.

Define It!

life cycle: the course of changes that happen during the life of a living thing

reproduce: to produce offspring

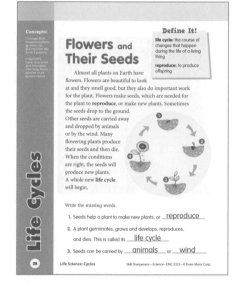

Write the missing words.

1. Seeds help a plant to make new plants, or reproduce
2. A plant germinates, grows and develops, reproduces, and dies. This is called its life cycle
3. Seeds can be carried by animals or wind

Life Cycles

28   Life Science: Cycles   Skill Sharpeners—Science • EMC 5323 • © Evan-Moor Corp.

Page 29

Insects Carry Pollen

Flowers make seeds when **pollen** travels from the **stamen** of a flower to the **pistil**. Insects such as bees, moths, and butterflies help carry pollen from one flower to another. When an insect lands on a flower, pollen sticks to the insect. When the insect visits another flower, some of the pollen falls off its body and **pollinates** that flower.

Define It!

pistil: the part of a flower in which seeds develop

pollen: tiny grains that help a plant produce seeds

pollinates: brings pollen to a plant

stamen: the part of a flower with pollen at the tip

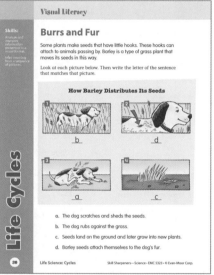

pistil — stamen
— petal

Number the events below in the correct order.

1 The bee lands on a flower to eat and drink.
3 The bee flies to another flower.
2 Pollen sticks to the bee.
5 The flower makes seeds.
4 Pollen falls off the bee.

Write the words to complete the sentence.

When a bee carries pollen from one flower to another, the bee pollinates the flower.

Life Cycles

© Evan-Moor Corp. • EMC 5323 • Skill Sharpeners—Science   Life Science: Cycles   29

Page 30

Visual Literacy

Burrs and Fur

Some plants make seeds that have little hooks. These hooks can attach to animals passing by. Barley is a type of grass plant that moves its seeds in this way.

Look at each picture below. Then write the letter of the sentence that matches that picture.

How Barley Distributes Its Seeds

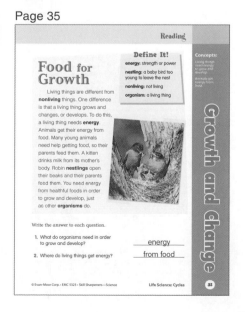

1 b   2 d
3 a   4 c

a. The dog scratches and sheds the seeds.
b. The dog rubs against the grass.
c. Seeds land on the ground and later grow into new plants.
d. Barley seeds attach themselves to the dog's fur.

Life Cycles

30   Life Science: Cycles   Skill Sharpeners—Science • EMC 5323 • © Evan-Moor Corp.

Page 31

Vocabulary Practice

Review the Words

Read each clue and write the missing word on the lines.

germinate   pollen   reproduce   stamen

1. The pistil and the s t a m e n are parts of a flower.
2. When conditions are right, a tiny seed will g e r m i n a t e
3. Tiny grains of p o l l e n stick to an insect.
4. Flowers r e p r o d u c e by making seeds.

Write the letters from the yellow boxes to answer the riddle.

Science Riddle

Where does a tiny plant hide?

inside every s e e d

Life Cycles

© Evan-Moor Corp. • EMC 5323 • Skill Sharpeners—Science   Life Science: Cycles   31

Page 34

Application

Life Cycle of a Plant

Look at the diagram of the life cycle of a plant. Describe each step of the life cycle on the lines below.

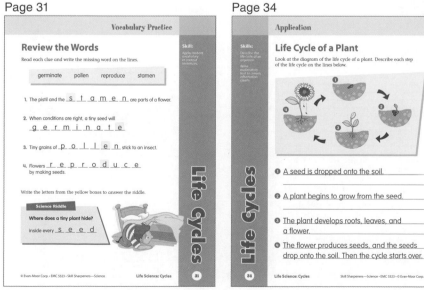

❶ A seed is dropped onto the soil.
❷ A plant begins to grow from the seed.
❸ The plant develops roots, leaves, and a flower.
❹ The flower produces seeds, and the seeds drop onto the soil. Then the cycle starts over.

Life Cycles

34   Life Science: Cycles   Skill Sharpeners—Science • EMC 5323 • © Evan-Moor Corp.

Page 35

Reading

Food for Growth

Living things are different from **nonliving** things. One difference is that a living thing grows and changes, or develops. To do this, a living thing needs **energy**. Animals get their energy from food. Many young animals need help getting food, so their parents feed them. A kitten drinks milk from its mother's body. Robin **nestlings** open their beaks and their parents feed them. You need energy from healthful foods in order to grow and develop, just as other **organisms** do.

Define It!

energy: strength or power

nestling: a baby bird too young to leave the nest

nonliving: not living

organism: a living thing

Write the answer to each question.

1. What do organisms need in order to grow and develop?   energy
2. Where do living things get energy?   from food

Growth and change

© Evan-Moor Corp. • EMC 5323 • Skill Sharpeners—Science   Life Science: Cycles   35

Growth and change

Fast and Slow Growth

Define It!
hatchling: a baby animal that has just hatched
mammal: a warm-blooded animal
offspring: an animal's young
reptile: a cold-blooded animal

Rabbits are **mammals** that grow and develop quickly. A baby rabbit grows in its mother's body for about a month before it is born. A baby rabbit is called a *kit*. Rabbit kits are born without fur. The kits leave the nest when they are only two weeks old. By six months old, a rabbit is an adult and can start its own family. Rabbits live for about nine years.

Turtles are **reptiles** that grow and develop slowly for years. Some types of turtles grow for 10 years before having **offspring**, and others might grow for 30 years. Turtle eggs hatch in about two to three months. **Hatchlings** are on their own at birth. Their shells are soft at first and do not protect them. The hatchlings must scurry off to hide in a safe place. Some turtles live for 120 years or more.

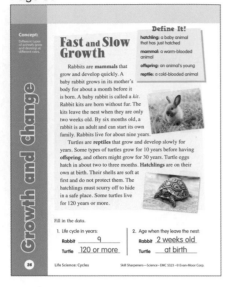

Fill in the data.

1. Life cycle in years:
   Rabbit __9__
   Turtle __120 or more__

2. Age when they leave the nest:
   Rabbit __2 weeks old__
   Turtle __at birth__

36 — Life Science: Cycles — Skill Sharpeners—Science • EMC 5323 • © Evan-Moor Corp.

Growth and change

Big Changes

Define It!
chrysalis: a hard shell
larva: a wingless insect form
metamorphosis: a series of changes
molt: to shed an outer covering
nymph: a young insect stage
pupa: an insect stage after larva

Some animals make a very big change as they develop. This change is called **metamorphosis**.

Butterfly: Complete Metamorphosis
A butterfly develops in four stages: egg, **larva**, **pupa**, and adult. The egg is laid on a plant. A caterpillar, or larva, hatches from the egg. The caterpillar then becomes a pupa. The pupa sticks to a twig and forms a hard shell called a **chrysalis**. In the spring, an adult butterfly pushes out of the chrysalis.

A butterfly is coming out of its chrysalis.

Dragonfly: Incomplete Metamorphosis
A dragonfly develops in three stages: egg, **nymph**, and adult. Dragonflies lay their eggs in water. When a nymph hatches from an egg, it does not have wings yet. The nymph grows and sheds its skin. This is called **molting**. The nymph molts many times before it grows wings and leaves the water to fly off.

A nymph is molting.

Circle *true* or *false*.

1. Both butterflies and dragonflies molt. true **(false)**
2. Butterflies and dragonflies go through metamorphosis. **(true)** false

© Evan-Moor Corp. • EMC 5323 • Skill Sharpeners—Science — Life Science: Cycles 37

Visual Literacy

What's Inside an Egg?

Chickens and other birds lay eggs in order to reproduce. A chicken egg holds the beginnings of growth.

Read about some of the parts of a chicken egg. Then label each part to complete the diagram.

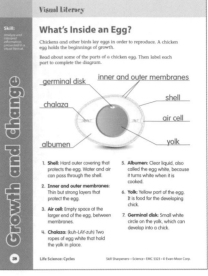

germinal disk — inner and outer membranes — shell — chalaza — air cell — albumen — yolk

1. **Shell:** Hard outer covering that protects the egg. Water and air can pass through the shell.
2. **Inner and outer membranes:** Thin but strong layers that protect the egg.
3. **Air cell:** Empty space at the larger end of the egg, between membranes.
4. **Chalaza:** (kuh-LAY-zuh) Two ropes of egg white that hold the yolk in place.
5. **Albumen:** Clear liquid, also called the egg white, because it turns white when it is cooked.
6. **Yolk:** Yellow part of the egg. It is food for the developing chick.
7. **Germinal disk:** Small white circle on the yolk, which can develop into a chick.

38 — Life Science: Cycles — Skill Sharpeners—Science • EMC 5323 • © Evan-Moor Corp.

Vocabulary Practice

Either/Or Questions

Write each answer.

1. Is an organism living **or** nonliving? — __living__
2. Is a nestling a kitten **or** a baby bird? — __baby bird__
3. Does energy come from food **or** a hard shell? — __food__
4. Is a rabbit a reptile **or** a mammal? — __mammal__
5. Are hatchlings a safe place **or** offspring? — __offspring__
6. Is metamorphosis a change **or** a chrysalis? — __change__
7. Is a chrysalis a hard shell **or** an adult insect? — __hard shell__
8. Does a nymph stick to a twig **or** molt? — __molt__
9. Is a reptile warm-blooded **or** cold-blooded? — __cold-blooded__
10. Is a caterpillar a larva **or** a mammal? — __larva__

Growth and change

© Evan-Moor Corp. • EMC 5323 • Skill Sharpeners—Science — Life Science: Cycles 39

Application

Hatchlings and Newborns

Read the clues about baby animals. Draw a line from the word to the picture. Then label the picture.

Did You Know?
Hatchlings and newborns are able to do different things for themselves. Some need their parents to feed and care for them. Others are on their own right away.

giraffe   human
duckling   sea turtle

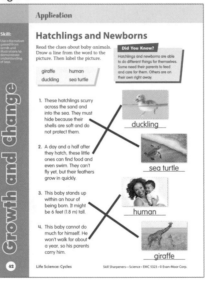

1. These hatchlings scurry across the sand and into the sea. They must hide because their shells are soft and do not protect them. → __sea turtle__

2. A day and a half after they hatch, these little ones can find food and even swim. They can't fly yet, but their feathers grow in quickly. → __duckling__

3. This baby stands within an hour of being born. It might be 6 feet (1.8 m) tall. → __giraffe__

4. This baby cannot do much for himself. He won't walk for about a year, so his parents carry him. → __human__

Growth and change

42 — Life Science: Cycles — Skill Sharpeners—Science • EMC 5323 • © Evan-Moor Corp.

Reading

Hunting Together for Food

Define It!
carnivore: a meat eater
herd: a group of animals that keep together
prey: an animal hunted for food
pride: a group of lions

Animals often live together in groups so they can help each other find food. Lions are a good example of this because they live in large families called **prides**. A pride might have 10 or 12 lions. Because they are **carnivores**, or meat eaters, lions must hunt for their food. Most of their **prey** can run faster than lions do. So lions work together to catch their prey. One mother lion circles a **herd** of zebras and hides in the tall grass. Another lion sneaks up close to the herd and then runs at a zebra. The frightened zebra runs toward the hiding lion. The lion comes out of hiding, jumps on the zebra, and brings it to the ground. Everyone in the pride shares the meat.

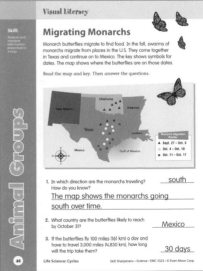

Circle *true* or *false*.

1. Lions hunt because they are carnivores. **(true)** false
2. Lions work together when they hunt. **(true)** false
3. Most of their prey cannot run as fast lions do. true **(false)**

Animal Groups

© Evan-Moor Corp. • EMC 5323 • Skill Sharpeners—Science — Life Science: Cycles 43

Guarding the Group

Define It!
attack: to move against with force
charge: to rush forward
rumbling: a long, low, heavy sound
trumpeting: a loud sound like a trumpet

African elephants travel in a herd. All of the elephants in the herd take care of each other. The leader of the herd is an old mother elephant. The other elephants follow her because she knows how to guard the family if danger appears.

Elephants talk to each other with sounds. Some sounds are so deep and **rumbling** that people cannot hear them. If danger comes near, the rumbling stops. Everyone is on guard. Mothers flap their ears to call their babies to them. The elephants circle around the baby elephants to guard them.

If a lion suddenly **attacks**, the elephants make **trumpeting** sounds and hit the ground with their trunks. The leader puts herself in front of the herd. She flaps her ears out to make herself look even larger. Then she lowers her head and **charges** the enemy in a big cloud of dust.

Write the missing words.

1. Elephants in a __herd__ take care of each other.
2. Elephants make __rumbling__ and __trumpeting__ sounds.
3. The leader guards the herd from __danger__.

Animal Groups

44 — Life Science: Cycles — Skill Sharpeners—Science • EMC 5323 • © Evan-Moor Corp.

Flocking Together

Define It!
flock: a group of birds together
habitat: a natural home
migrate: to move from one habitat to another
raft: a group of ducks on water
wedge: birds flying in a V-shape

Have you ever seen a **raft** of ducks swimming or a **wedge** of geese flying? Those are names for **flocks** of birds. Why do birds flock together? Some birds feed in a group because it is easier to find food. If one bird finds food, all can feed on it.

Sometimes birds flock together when their **habitat** changes. When the seasons change from summer to fall, the berries, seeds, and bugs that birds eat are harder to find. So birds **migrate** south to warmer places that have more food. Geese, ducks, and swans fly together in a **wedge**, or V-shape, when they migrate. They honk to let each other know where they are. Even at night or in cloudy skies, they can keep together.

1. Why do some birds migrate? __to find food in a warmer habitat__
2. How does a wedge of geese talk to each other? __They honk.__

Animal Groups

© Evan-Moor Corp. • EMC 5323 • Skill Sharpeners—Science — Life Science: Cycles 45

Visual Literacy

Migrating Monarchs

Monarch butterflies migrate to find food. In the fall, swarms of monarchs migrate from places in the U.S. They come together in Texas and continue on to Mexico. The key shows symbols for dates. The map shows where the butterflies are on those dates.

Read the map and key. Then answer the questions.

Monarch Migration Routes
▲ Sept. 27 – Oct. 3
● Oct. 4 – Oct. 10
★ Oct. 11 – Oct. 17

1. In which direction are the monarchs traveling? How do you know? — __south__
   __The map shows the monarchs going south over time.__
2. What country are the butterflies likely to reach by October 31? — __Mexico__
3. If the butterflies fly 100 miles (161 km) a day and have to travel 3,000 miles (4,830 km), how long will the trip take them? — __30 days__

Animal Groups

46 — Life Science: Cycles — Skill Sharpeners—Science • EMC 5323 • © Evan-Moor Corp.

Animal Groups Crossword Puzzle

Use the vocabulary words to complete the crossword puzzle.

habitat | carnivore | charge | pride | prey
trumpeting | rumbling | flock | migrate

Across
2. an animal hunted for food
5. to rush forward
6. a long, low, heavy sound
7. to move from one habitat to another
9. a meat eater

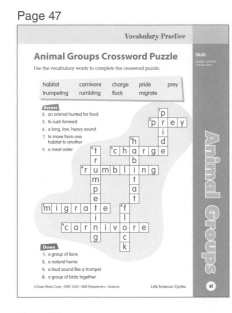

Down
1. a group of lions
3. a natural home
4. a loud sound like a trumpet
8. a group of birds together

How Young Animals Survive

Define It!
cub: a young bear
female: able to lay eggs or give birth to young
offspring: the young of an animal
sow: an adult female bear
survive: to stay alive

Animal babies are called **offspring**. The offspring of some animals must **survive** on their own. For example, the parents of a baby turtle, or turtle hatchling, are not around to keep it safe from bigger animals. **Female** turtles lay hundreds of eggs, but only some offspring will survive.

A black bear has fewer offspring. A female black bear, or **sow**, gives birth to two or three **cubs** in the middle of winter. The cubs are ready to leave their warm den in the spring. But the cubs stay close to their mother. She keeps them safe and teaches them to climb a tree quickly to get out of danger. The sow shows her cubs which plants, berries, and insects to eat. When the cubs are one and a half years old, they leave their mother to survive on their own.

Write the answer to each question.

1. Many turtle hatchlings do not survive. Why? _Their parents are not around to keep them safe._

2. How long do black bear cubs live with their mother? _one and a half years_

Parents and Offspring

Define It!
cygnet: a young swan
inherit: to get from a parent
pen: an adult female swan
resemble: to be or look like
trait: a feature belonging to a living thing

Young animals grow up to **resemble**, or look like, their parents. Do you know the fairy tale called "The Ugly Duckling"? In that story, a baby hatches from an egg, but it doesn't look like the mother duck. Later in the story, the baby grows into a beautiful swan. A swan's egg had somehow gotten into a duck's nest! Ducklings grow into ducks and **cygnets** grow into swans.

Offspring **inherit** some of their **traits**, or looks, from each of their parents. Some traits appear as the young animal grows. Compare the traits of the cygnets and the **pen** (mother swan) in this picture.

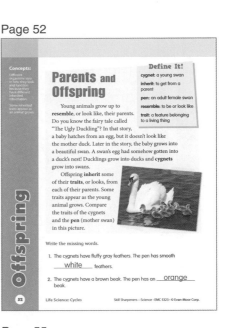

Write the missing words.

1. The cygnets have fluffy gray feathers. The pen has smooth _white_ feathers.

2. The cygnets have a brown beak. The pen has an _orange_ beak.

From Egg to Frog

Define It!
froglet: a tiny frog
gills: body parts of a water animal
hind: at the back
lungs: body parts for breathing air
tadpole: a newly hatched frog

Life Cycle of a Frog

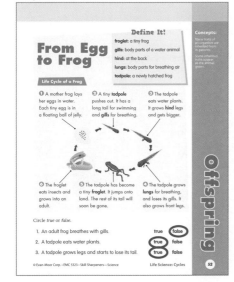

1. A mother frog lays her eggs in water. Each tiny egg is in a floating ball of jelly.
2. A tiny **tadpole** pushes out. It has a long tail for swimming and **gills** for breathing.
3. The tadpole eats water plants. It grows **hind** legs and gets bigger.
4. The froglet eats insects and grows into an adult.
5. The tadpole has become a tiny **froglet**. It jumps onto land. The rest of its tail will soon be gone.
6. The tadpole grows **lungs** for breathing, and loses its gills. It also grows front legs.

Circle *true* or *false*.

1. An adult frog breathes with gills. true **false**
2. A tadpole eats water plants. **true** false
3. A tadpole grows legs and starts to lose its tail. **true** false

---

Are You My Parent?

Did You Know?
Offspring resemble their parents. There are many kinds of apes and monkeys. Most monkeys have tails, while apes do not. The hair, face, coloring, and arms or legs of the animals help to tell them apart, too.

Draw a line to match the parent with its offspring. Use the list of traits to help you. Make a check mark by each trait as you make a match.

chimpanzee | orangutan | squirrel monkey

___ face   ___ ears   ___ coloring
___ tail   ___ face   ___ arms
___ coloring   ___ hair   ___ face

Review the Words

Read each clue and write the missing word on the lines.

trait | cygnet | tadpole | cub | hind

1. A young frog with gills and a tail is a _t a d p o l e_
2. The offspring of a swan is a _c y g n e t_
3. A frog's _h i n d_ legs grow before its front legs do.
4. A colorful beak is a _t r a i t_ of some adult swans.
5. A black bear _c u b_ stays with its mother for one and a half years.

Write the letters from the yellow boxes to answer the riddle.

Science Riddle

What lives in a little house and must break through the wall to go out?

a _b a b y c h i c k_

Fossils

Define It!
decay: to break down or rot
fossil: remains or marks of a living thing that lived long ago
mineral: something found in nature that is not plant or animal
sediment: soil or sand that forms layers on land or under water

A **fossil** is the remains or marks of a plant or an animal that lived long ago. Living things **decay** when they die. But if their bones, shells, or teeth are buried quickly by **sediment**, a fossil can form. Over millions of years, heavy layers of sediment pile up and harden into rock.

A **mold** is one kind of fossil. It is made when a plant or an animal rots away and leaves only its shape in the rock.

A **cast** is another kind of fossil. It is made when **minerals** fill a mold in the same shape as the plant or animal.

A **trace fossil** is made from things such as footprints or nests. They tell scientists how the animals moved and lived.

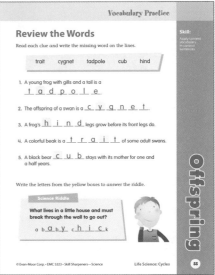

mold
cast
dinosaur's footprint

Check the box that answers the question.

1. Which of these would **not** make a trace fossil?
   ☐ footprint   ☑ bone   ☐ nest

2. Which of these could show the entire shape of an animal?
   ☐ sediment   ☐ trace fossil   ☑ cast

The Fossil Record

Define It!
extinct: no longer to be found living
fossil record: the history of life on Earth as told by fossils
marker fossil: fossil that marks a time in the fossil record
trilobite: an extinct sea animal

The layers of rock on Earth have built up over time. Scientists try to understand what Earth was like long ago by studying fossils in the different layers of rock. Scientists call Earth's layers of rock the **fossil record**.

Trilobite fossils are common in the fossil record. Trilobites were sea animals that lived about 250 million to 540 million years ago. They are now **extinct**, or no longer to be found. These extinct animals are useful to scientists today. Trilobites are **marker fossils**. When a new kind of fossil is discovered, scientists want to figure out when that plant or animal lived. The fossil record can tell scientists if the organism lived before, after, or at the same time as trilobites.

Write the missing words.

1. Trilobites are _extinct_ sea animals that had three main body parts.

2. The layers of rock in the _fossil record_ give clues about when an organism lived.

Earth's Past

Define It!
continents: the seven largest bodies of land on Earth
fern: a feathery plant
landmass: a large body of land

The story of Earth's past tells of big changes over millions of years. Fossils are clues that tell how life on Earth changed over time. Fossils of a **fern** plant gave scientists a clue. The same fossils were found on different **continents**. The scientists began to think that the continents were once connected. Now scientists think that all the continents were one giant **landmass** about 200 million years ago. They call that landmass Pangaea (pan-JEE-uh).

Today, millions of years after Pangaea broke apart, the continents are still moving very slowly. The movement of continents builds mountains. When two continents push into each other, their rock layers push together and make a mountain. Sometimes the layers are pushed up all the way from the ocean floor. If those rock layers hold fossils, the fossils travel up with the rocks. This is why fossils of sea animals have been found at the tops of mountains.

Circle *true* or *false*.

1. Earth has always looked the way it does now. true **false**
2. Fossils can tell us what Earth looked like long ago. **true** false
3. Sea animal fossils cannot be found on a mountain. true **false**

Page 62

Visual Literacy

Skills: Infer meaning from pictures. Classify events in sequential order.

Stuck in Time

Scientists have been digging up thousands of fossils in the city of Los Angeles, California! The area is called the La Brea (lah BRAY-uh) Tar Pits. Scientists have found the bones of mammoths and saber-toothed cats there. These extinct animals were trapped in the tar pits about 30,000 years ago.

Write the letter of the sentence that matches each picture.

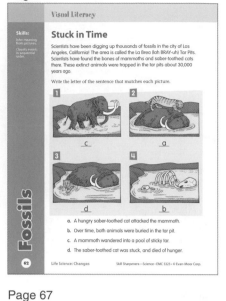

1 c
2 a
3 d
4 b

a. A hungry saber-toothed cat attacked the mammoth.

b. Over time, both animals were buried in the tar pit.

c. A mammoth wandered into a pool of sticky tar.

d. The saber-toothed cat was stuck, and died of hunger.

Fossils

62 · Life Science: Changes · Skill Sharpeners—Science • EMC 5323 · © Evan-Moor Corp.

Page 63

Vocabulary Practice

Skill: Apply content vocabulary.

Fossils Crossword Puzzle

Use the vocabulary words to complete the crossword puzzle.

decay   fossil   trilobite   landmass
continents   extinct   sediment   fern

Across
4. the seven largest bodies of land on Earth
6. soil or sand that forms layers on land or underwater
8. no longer found to be living

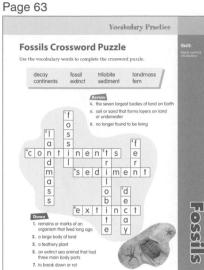

Down
1. remains or marks of an organism that lived long ago
2. a large body of land
3. a feathery plant
5. an extinct sea animal that had three main body parts
7. to break down or rot

Fossils

© Evan-Moor Corp. · EMC 5323 · Skill Sharpeners—Science · Life Science: Changes · 63

Page 66

Application

Skill: Apply scientific knowledge to write a narrative about an imagined experience.

Fossil Discovery

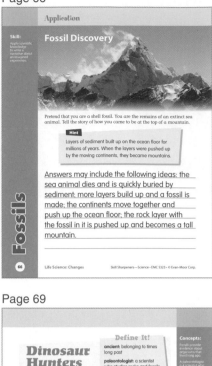

Pretend that you are a shell fossil. You are the remains of an extinct sea animal. Tell the story of how you came to be at the top of a mountain.

Hint
Layers of sediment built up on the ocean floor for millions of years. When the layers were pushed up by the moving continents, they became mountains.

Answers may include the following ideas: the sea animal dies and is quickly buried by sediment; more layers build up and a fossil is made; the continents move together and push up the ocean floor; the rock layer with the fossil in it is pushed up and becomes a tall mountain.

Fossils

66 · Life Science: Changes · Skill Sharpeners—Science • EMC 5323 · © Evan-Moor Corp.

Page 67

Reading

The Dinosaurs

Define It!
armor: a hard covering
hind: at the back or rear
prey: an animal hunted for food
reptiles: animals with a backbone and scales
survive: to continue to live

Concepts: Some kinds of animals that once lived on Earth are no longer found anywhere. Dinosaurs had bodies that were built to help them survive.

Dinosaurs were **reptiles** that lived on Earth long ago for about 160 million years. How did they **survive** for so long?

One answer is that their bodies were built to help them survive. Meat-eating dinosaurs like *Tyrannosaurus rex* (tuh-RAN-no-SOHR-uhs reks) had two short legs in front. They traveled on their two **hind** legs. Meat eaters had big jaws and sharp teeth. They had hands with sharp claws to catch and hold their **prey**.

Some plant-eating dinosaurs were giants. *Diplodocus* (deh-PLAH-duh-kuhs) was about 90 feet (27 m) long, with a small head and a long neck. These dinosaurs moved on four feet because of their large size. Their size could scare away meat-eating dinosaurs.

Other plant-eating dinosaurs had **armor** to protect them. They had bony plates, horns, and spikes. *Triceratops* had head armor. *Stegosaurus* (STEG-uh-SOHR-uhs) could swing its spiked tail to strike an enemy.

Tyrannosaurus rex (T. rex)
Diplodocus
Stegosaurus

Write the missing words.

1. Meat-eating dinosaurs had big jaws and ___sharp teeth___.

2. Some plant-eating dinosaurs had ___armor___ such as bony plates, horns, and spikes.

Dinosaurs

© Evan-Moor Corp. · EMC 5323 · Skill Sharpeners—Science · Life Science: Changes · 67

Page 68

Concept: The fossil record provides evidence about dinosaurs and their disappearance.

Dinosaurs Disappear

Define It!
asteroid: a small rocky body that travels around the sun
crater: a bowl-shaped hole
fossil record: layers of rock containing fossils

Although dinosaurs were the main form of animal life for millions of years, they died out about 65 million years ago. We know this because there are no dinosaur fossils in the **fossil record** after that time. What happened that caused the dinosaurs to disappear? Scientists have been asking that same question.

One idea is that a large space rock, called an **asteroid**, hit Earth. Today in Mexico there is a giant hole more than 100 miles (161 km) across. Scientists think an asteroid made this **crater**. When the asteroid hit Earth, it caused large amounts of dust to rise into the air. It started huge fires, too. The smoke and dust blocked out the sun. Plants could not live without sunlight. Plant-eating dinosaurs could not live without plants. And meat eaters died when their prey were gone.

Answer each question.

1. When did the dinosaurs die out? ___65 million years ago___

2. What made a huge crater in Mexico? ___an asteroid___

3. Without the sun, living things ___could not live___

Dinosaurs

68 · Life Science: Changes · Skill Sharpeners—Science • EMC 5323 · © Evan-Moor Corp.

Page 69

Define It!
ancient: belonging to times long past
paleontologist: a scientist who studies rocks and fossils to learn about living things of the past

Dinosaur Hunters

Concepts: Fossils provide evidence about organisms that lived long ago. A paleontologist is a scientist who studies living things of the ancient past.

Dinosaurs lived long before people did. About 200 years ago, people did not know about dinosaurs and their **ancient** world. If fossils were found, people did not know what they were. Then, in the early 1800s, science-minded people started to look at fossils differently. Scientists began to think that the large teeth and bones they found belonged to a new kind of animal. In 1842, Sir Richard Owen named the new group of animals *dinosaurs*, which means "terrible lizards." Dinosaurs were not lizards, but the name *dinosaur* has stuck. A new science was born that studied living things of long ago. Today, scientists called **paleontologists** (PAY-lee-ahn-TAHL-uh-jists) are using rocks and fossils to learn more about living things of the ancient past.

Triceratops

Circle *true* or *false*.

1. Dinosaurs lived until the 1800s.   true **false**
2. Dinosaurs were giant lizards.   true **false**
3. Paleontologists study the ancient past.   **true** false

Dinosaurs

© Evan-Moor Corp. · EMC 5323 · Skill Sharpeners—Science · Life Science: Changes · 69

Page 70

Visual Literacy

Skills: Analyze and interpret information presented in an illustration. Gather and record scientific data in a table or chart.

Bird or Dinosaur?

Many scientists think that birds are modern-day relatives of dinosaurs. The scientists see many things about the bodies of birds and dinosaurs that are alike. For example, scientists think that *Tyrannosaurus rex* ran on its toes, just as many birds do.

Compare the pictures of a dinosaur's foot and a bird's foot. Write your data in the chart.

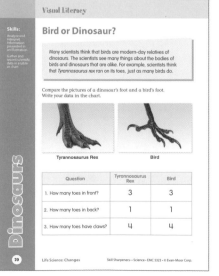

Tyrannosaurus Rex   Bird

Question	Tyrannosaurus Rex	Bird
1. How many toes in front?	3	3
2. How many toes in back?	1	1
3. How many toes have claws?	4	4

Dinosaurs

70 · Life Science: Changes · Skill Sharpeners—Science • EMC 5323 · © Evan-Moor Corp.

Page 71

Vocabulary Practice

Skill: Apply content vocabulary.

Either/Or Questions

Write each answer.

1. Is something that is ancient new **or** old? ___old___

2. Is prey an animal that hunts **or** one that is hunted? ___is hunted___

3. Is armor hard **or** soft? ___hard___

4. Is an asteroid an animal **or** a rock? ___rock___

5. Is a paleontologist a person **or** a dinosaur? ___person___

6. Is a crater a hole **or** an asteroid? ___hole___

7. Is a hind leg in front **or** in back? ___in back___

8. Have birds survived **or** died out? ___survived___

9. Was a dinosaur a reptile **or** a mammal? ___reptile___

Dinosaurs

© Evan-Moor Corp. · EMC 5323 · Skill Sharpeners—Science · Life Science: Changes · 71

Page 75

Reading

Dolphin Adaptations

Define It!
adaptation: a feature that helps a living thing stay alive
blowhole: an opening on the top of the head used for breathing
survive: to stay alive
trait: a feature belonging to a living thing

Concept: External characteristics of living things allow their needs to be met.

Living things have **traits**, or features. A trait that helps a living thing **survive** is called an **adaptation**. Dolphins have a special adaptation that helps them breathe underwater. A dolphin breathes through a **blowhole** on the top of its head, instead of through a nose or mouth like ours. The dolphin uses strong muscles to open its blowhole when it swims to the water's surface. As it dives underwater, the blowhole closes.

Dolphins have other adaptations, too. They have a tail and two flippers. They swim through the water by moving their tail and steering with their flippers.

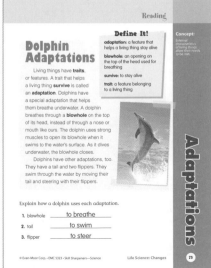

Explain how a dolphin uses each adaptation.

1. blowhole ___to breathe___
2. tail ___to swim___
3. flipper ___to steer___

Adaptations

© Evan-Moor Corp. · EMC 5323 · Skill Sharpeners—Science · Life Science: Changes · 75

Page 76

Rock Pocket Mouse

Color is an adaptation that helps animals survive. When animals hide by blending in with the things around them, it is called **camouflage**. The rock pocket mouse is an example of camouflage. This mouse lived in the desert. Its sandy-brown color blended in with the sand and rocks and camouflaged the mouse. Owls and other animals that eat mice couldn't easily see it, so the rock pocket mice had a good chance of surviving. Then, long ago, **lava** from a **volcano** flowed over part of the desert. The lava cooled into dark rock. The light-colored mice were no longer safe on the dark rocks. By chance, a few dark-colored mice were born. The dark-colored mice survived, and the light-colored mice were eaten. More dark mice were born. Now, almost all of the rock pocket mice living on the dark rocks are dark-colored. And the mice living in the sandy part of the desert are light-colored.

Define It!

camouflage: colors that hide an animal

lava: melted rock

volcano: an opening in the earth where lava flows out

Answer the questions.

1. How does the rock pocket mouse hide? with camouflage

2. Which mice survive on the dark rocks? the dark-colored mice

Page 77

Cactus Spines

A cactus has adaptations that help it survive in a hot, dry desert. One adaptation is its needles, or **spines**. A spine is an adaptation of a leaf. Spines can be useful in different ways. Spines catch water and drip it toward the roots of the cactus. A cactus may be thickly covered with spines that shade it and keep it from drying out in the sun. Some spines **protect** a cactus from animals looking for a juicy meal. The animals learn that the spines will stick in their mouth, so they keep away. The jumping cholla (CHOY-ah) cactus uses its spines to **reproduce**. If an animal brushes against a jumping cholla, a small piece breaks off and sticks to the animal. In time, the piece drops to the ground, grows roots, and becomes a new plant.

Define It!

protect: to keep safe

reproduce: to produce offspring

spines: the stiff, sharp needles of a cactus

Circle *true* or *false*.

1. A cactus spine adapted from a leaf. (true) false

2. Spines are not very useful to a cactus. true (false)

3. One type of cactus uses its spines to make new plants. (true) false

Page 78

Visual Literacy

Barrel Cactus

Cactus spines catch water to help a cactus survive. The barrel cactus has other adaptations that help it get and store water. The roots of the cactus spread out like a net to quickly drink up even the smallest amount of desert rain. A barrel cactus has folds that can swell and store gallons or liters of water. Its thick, waxy skin keeps the water inside the plant from escaping into the air.

Label the diagram to show four adaptations of the barrel cactus. Use the words below.

roots   folds   spines   thick, waxy skin

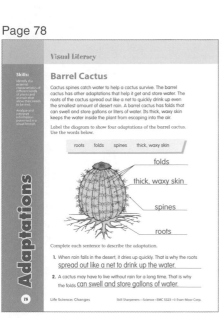

folds
thick, waxy skin
spines
roots

Complete each sentence to describe the adaptation.

1. When rain falls in the desert, it dries up quickly. That is why the roots spread out like a net to drink up the water.

2. A cactus may have to live without rain for a long time. That is why the folds can swell and store gallons of water.

Page 79

Vocabulary Practice

Review the Words

Read each clue and write the missing word on the lines.

| camouflage | volcano | adaptation |
| blowhole | spines | survive |

1. A dolphin breathes through its
b l o w h o l e

2. The dark color of a rock pocket mouse is an
a d a p t a t i o n

3. The sharp needles of a cactus are called
s p i n e s

4. Adaptations help living things s u r v i v e

5. Animals use c a m o u f l a g e to help them hide.

6. Lava flows from a v o l c a n o

Write the letters from the yellow boxes to answer the riddle.

Science Riddle

What is a mouse's favorite game?

h i de and s q u e a k

Page 80

Hands-on Activity

Plant Adaptation

A cactus can store water for months. But not all plants have this adaptation. See what happens to a celery stalk with and without water.

What You Need
- celery stalk
- paper towel
- water in a glass
- an adult to cut the celery

What You Do

1. Have an adult cut off the bottom of the celery stalk. Notice the tiny holes at the bottom. These are tiny tubes that go up the stalk.

2. Set the stalk on a paper towel and leave it out overnight.

3. Look at the celery stalk. Notice how it looks and feels now.

4. Stand the celery in the glass of water, with the cut end at the bottom. Leave it like this overnight.

5. Now look at the celery stalk. Notice how it looks and feels.

What Did You Discover?

Answers will vary. Examples:

1. Describe how the celery looked and felt after being on the paper towel.
It was limp.

2. Describe how the celery looked and felt after being in water overnight.
It looked straight and felt firm.

3. Compare the celery with a cactus. Write one way they are alike and one way they are different.
They both drink up and store water.
A cactus has spinces but celery does not.

Page 83

Reading

Iguana in the Ocean

An **ecosystem** is made up of nonliving and living things in their **habitats**. When one thing changes, it **affects** the others.

The Galápagos (guh-LAH-puh-gohs) Islands are a special ecosystem because many of the animals that live there are not found anywhere else. One such animal is a lizard called the Galápagos **iguana**. All lizards are land animals except for these iguanas. They swim into the ocean to eat tiny **algae** that grow there. Then they return to land to warm up in the sun. During some years, the ocean gets warmer and there is less algae to eat. When this happens, the iguanas are affected. The bones in their bodies shrink in size. Their smaller bodies warm up in the sun more quickly, so they can make more trips to feed in the water. When the ocean gets colder again, the iguanas grow larger.

Define It!

affect: to make a difference to

algae: tiny water plants

ecosystem: a community of living and nonliving things that have an effect on each other

habitat: a home in nature

iguana: a type of lizard

Answer the questions.

1. What happens in the iguana's habitat that changes its food supply?
The ocean gets warmer.

2. How do the iguanas change? Their bones get smaller.

Page 84

Brown Tree Snakes

Without knowing it, people changed the ecosystem on the island of Guam (gwahm). Brown tree snakes slipped in more than 60 years ago. They were hiding in the wheels of **military** planes and on **cargo** boats. Now there are more than two million brown tree snakes on Guam. The snakes have caused big changes to the ecosystem. There used to be many forest birds, but the snakes ate them. Now birds are nearly all gone, and some **species** of birds are **extinct**. Because there are fewer birds to eat spiders, there are many more spiders. There are not enough birds to help spread seeds, so fewer new trees and plants grow in the forest. Scientists are working to find ways to get rid of the snakes without harming other parts of the ecosystem.

Define It!

cargo: goods carried on a ship

extinct: no longer to be found living

military: armed forces

species: a group of plants or animals that have many common traits

Circle *true* or *false*.

1. There are millions of snakes on Guam. (true) false

2. Birds are nearly gone from Guam. (true) false

3. Spiders are extinct species on Guam. true (false)

Page 85

Paperbark Trees

People brought paperbark trees from Australia to Florida, and the trees changed Florida's ecosystem. People planted paperbark trees in Florida in the 1880s, hoping the trees could help dry out swampy land. But the paperbark trees took over, blocking out light and making it impossible for Florida's **native** plants to grow. Without the native plants, many animal and insect species could not survive. Unfortunately, very few animal species can live in the paperbark tree's habitat.

Another problem is that the trees **survive** Florida's **wildfires** but Florida's native plants do not. So, there are fewer native plants and more paperbark trees. It is a very big problem to **control** the spread of these trees. Scientists know that this tree changes the ecosystem in Florida and makes native plant and animal species disappear.

Define It!

control: to reduce the number

native: belonging to a place

survive: to continue to live

wildfire: a fire that destroys a wide area

Answer the questions.

1. Why are Florida's native plants important? They give food and shelter to many animal and insect species.

2. What problem do scientists have? They need to control the spread of paperbark trees.

Page 86

Visual Literacy

Birds on the Move

Earth changes are happening. As Earth grows warmer, the ecosystems in which birds find food are changing, too. For forty years, scientists kept track of where birds live. By 2010, the habitats of birds in America had moved north. This graph shows the distance in miles and kilometers.

Look at the graph and answer the questions.

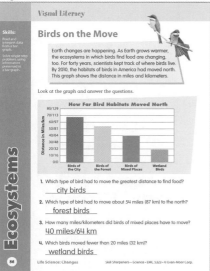

How Far Bird Habitats Moved North

Distance in Miles/km

1. Which type of bird had to move the greatest distance to find food?
city birds

2. Which type of bird had to move about 54 miles (87 km) to the north?
forest birds

3. How many miles/kilometers did birds of mixed places have to move?
40 miles/64 km

4. Which birds moved fewer than 20 miles (32 km)?
wetland birds

Page 87

Ecosystems Crossword Puzzle

Use the vocabulary words to complete the crossword puzzle.

iguana   species   native   ecosystem
wildfire   affect   extinct   algae

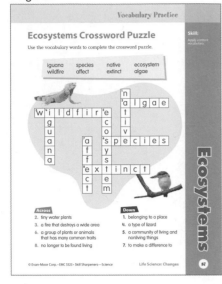

Across
2. tiny water plants
3. a fire that destroys a wide area
6. a group of plants or animals that has many common traits
8. no longer to be found living

Down
1. belonging to a place
4. a type of lizard
5. a community of living and nonliving things
7. to make a difference to

© Evan-Moor Corp. • EMC 5323 • Skill Sharpeners—Science · Life Science: Changes · 87

Page 91

The Atmosphere

Layers of **gases** circle Earth and stretch for hundreds of miles or kilometers above it. These layers are the **atmosphere**. The air we breathe is part of the atmosphere. The atmosphere is where **weather** happens. Weather is what is happening in the atmosphere in a certain place and time. Weather changes as the atmosphere changes.

One of the jobs of the atmosphere is to soak up heat from the sun's rays. It must also let some of the heat go back into space. This is how the atmosphere keeps Earth's **temperatures** from becoming too hot or too cold.

People can't change the weather, but we can measure it. We measure temperature with a **thermometer**. It tells us how hot or cold the air is.

Define It!
- **atmosphere:** layers of gases that circle Earth
- **gas:** matter that is not liquid or solid
- **temperature:** hotness or coldness
- **thermometer:** a tool that measures temperature
- **weather:** what happens in the atmosphere

Circle *true* or *false*.

1. Weather happens in the atmosphere.   (**true**) false
2. The atmosphere does not change.   true (**false**)
3. Temperature can be measured.   (**true**) false

© Evan-Moor Corp. • EMC 5323 • Skill Sharpeners—Science · Earth Science: Earth and Sky · 91

Page 92

Precipitation

The atmosphere holds water in the form of **water vapor**. Water vapor is made when water **evaporates**, or changes from a liquid to a gas. The vapor disappears into the air. If water vapor is lifted high enough into the air, it cools. Cooling causes the water vapor to **condense**, or form tiny drops of water. This is how clouds are formed. The tiny drops grow and change inside the clouds until they become so heavy that they fall to the ground as **precipitation**. Rain, snow, sleet, and hail are all types of precipitation. Scientists use a **rain gauge** to measure the rain that falls in a place.

Define It!
- **condense:** to change from a gas to a liquid form
- **evaporate:** to change into a gas
- **precipitation:** water that falls as rain, snow, sleet, or hail
- **rain gauge:** a tool that measures rainfall
- **water vapor:** the gas that clouds are made of

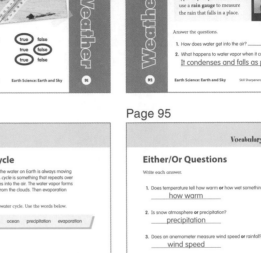

rain   snow   sleet   hail

Answer the questions.

1. How does water get into the air?   It evaporates.
2. What happens to water vapor when it cools?
   It condenses and falls as precipitation.

92 · Earth Science: Earth and Sky · Skill Sharpeners—Science · EMC 5323 · © Evan-Moor Corp.

Page 93

Wind

Meteorologists are scientists who study weather and **predict** its changes. Changes in the weather happen when the wind changes speed and direction. That is why meteorologists use special tools to measure wind speed and direction.

A **wind vane** is a tool that points in the direction the wind is blowing from. Another tool, called an **anemometer** (ann-ih-MOM-uh-tur), is used to measure how fast the wind is blowing. The faster the anemometer spins, the faster the wind is blowing. Without these tools, it would be difficult to measure the wind. It would also be difficult to know how strong a storm is, or to know in which direction it is moving.

Define It!
- **anemometer:** a tool that measures wind speed
- **meteorologist:** a scientist who studies the atmosphere and weather
- **predict:** to say what will happen in the future
- **wind vane:** a tool that shows wind direction

wind vane

anemometer

Write the tool that each person would use.

1. Maria wants to know in which direction the wind is blowing.   wind vane
2. Craig wants to measure how fast the wind is blowing.   anemometer
3. Rachel wants to know if the wind is traveling east or west.   wind vane

© Evan-Moor Corp. • EMC 5323 • Skill Sharpeners—Science · Earth Science: Earth and Sky · 93

Page 94

The Water Cycle

This diagram shows how the water on Earth is always moving through the water cycle. A cycle is something that repeats over and over. Water evaporates into the air. The water vapor forms clouds. Precipitation falls from the clouds. Then evaporation happens again.

Label the diagram of the water cycle. Use the words below.

land   sun   clouds   ocean   precipitation   evaporation

sun
clouds
precipitation
evaporation
land
ocean

94 · Earth Science: Earth and Sky · Skill Sharpeners—Science · EMC 5323 · © Evan-Moor Corp.

Page 95

Either/Or Questions

Write each answer.

1. Does temperature tell how warm **or** how wet something is?
   how warm
2. Is snow atmosphere **or** precipitation?
   precipitation
3. Does an anemometer measure wind speed **or** rainfall?
   wind speed
4. Does a thermometer measure wind direction **or** hot and cold?
   hot and cold
5. Does a meteorologist predict the weather **or** study rocks?
   predict the weather
6. Is water vapor in the ocean **or** the atmosphere?
   atmosphere
7. Can water predict **or** evaporate?
   evaporate
8. Are clouds formed by water vapor **or** a wind vane?
   water vapor

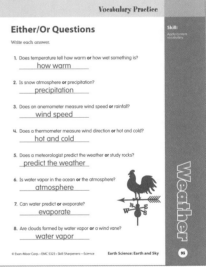

© Evan-Moor Corp. • EMC 5323 • Skill Sharpeners—Science · Earth Science: Earth and Sky · 95

Page 99

Climate and Weather

How are **climate** and **weather** different? Weather is what is happening now in the **atmosphere** in a certain place. Climate is the weather over a long period of time in a certain place. One day the weather might be cloudy or rainy in a city, but that city could have a dry, **desert** climate. Or the weather could be sunny and dry one day in a city that has a wet, **tropical** climate. Unlike the weather, which may change from one day to the next, climate does not change quickly. Changes in climate happen slowly over hundreds, thousands, and even millions of years.

Define It!
- **atmosphere:** layers of air that circle Earth
- **climate:** weather over a long period
- **desert:** a dry climate with little rainfall
- **tropical:** a climate where it rains almost every day and stays warm all year-round
- **weather:** what happens in the atmosphere

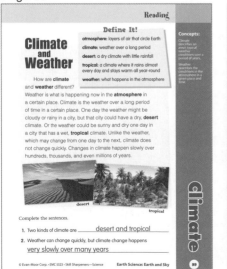

desert   tropical

Complete the sentences.

1. Two kinds of climate are   desert and tropical
2. Weather can change quickly, but climate change happens   very slowly over many years

© Evan-Moor Corp. • EMC 5323 · Skill Sharpeners—Science · Earth Science: Earth and Sky · 99

Page 100

Earth Is a Greenhouse

What is a **greenhouse** like on a cool winter's day? It's warm enough inside to grow plants, because a greenhouse is made of glass. The rays of the sun warm the inside, and the glass keeps the warmth in. Earth is like a greenhouse. The **gases** of the atmosphere trap the sun's warmth and keep Earth warm. These gases are sometimes called *greenhouse gases*. Scientists say that Earth's greenhouse is warming up too quickly because people are putting more greenhouse gases into the atmosphere. **Carbon dioxide** is a greenhouse gas that comes from burning **fuels**. When people use fuels for things such as running more cars and heating more buildings, then more carbon dioxide goes into the atmosphere. Scientists think that the extra gases are causing Earth's climate to change.

Define It!
- **carbon dioxide:** a gas found in the atmosphere
- **fuel:** material that is burned to make heat or power
- **gas:** matter that is not liquid or solid
- **greenhouse:** a glass building

Circle *true* or *false*.

1. Carbon dioxide is a gas in the atmosphere.   (**true**) false
2. Burning fuels makes carbon dioxide.   (**true**) false
3. Earth's greenhouse is cooling quickly.   true (**false**)

100 · Earth Science: Earth and Sky · Skill Sharpeners—Science · EMC 5323 · © Evan-Moor Corp.

Page 101

Coral Reefs in Trouble

A **coral reef** is a rocky form made from the hard parts of tiny animals called *corals*. Some reefs can stretch for hundreds of miles or kilometers in warm, shallow ocean waters. Octopuses, sea stars, sea turtles, and many kinds of fish are at home in the **ecosystem** of a coral reef. Scientists have noticed that some coral reefs are not healthy. The reefs are losing their beautiful pinks, oranges, purples, and other colors. This is called **bleaching**. It happens when the ocean becomes too warm for the **algae** that live inside the corals. Without the algae, the corals bleach and die. Scientists think that extra greenhouse gases are causing the oceans to warm up, and this harms the coral reefs.

Define It!
- **algae:** tiny water plants
- **bleach:** to turn white
- **coral reef:** a rocky form made from coral
- **ecosystem:** a community of living and nonliving things that affect each other

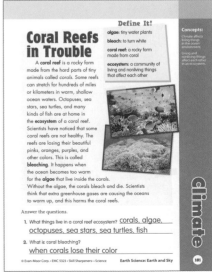

Answer the questions.

1. What things live in a coral reef ecosystem?   corals, algae, octopuses, sea stars, sea turtles, fish
2. What is coral bleaching?   when corals lose their color

© Evan-Moor Corp. • EMC 5323 · Skill Sharpeners—Science · Earth Science: Earth and Sky · 101

Page 102

Kinds of Climates

Skill: Use information gained from pictures and the words in a text to demonstrate understanding of the text.

Earth has many different kinds of climates, and scientists have given them different names. The pictures below show four kinds of climates. Read about each kind.

desert A dry climate with very little rain. Clear skies with no clouds make days hot and nights cold.

tropical It is hot and wet all year-round. Rainforests grow in this climate.

highland The climate changes as you climb the mountain. It can be hot and wet at the bottom and cold and dry at the top.

tundra A dry climate with cold all year-round. No trees can grow in the ground that is always frozen.

Write the name of the climate below each picture.

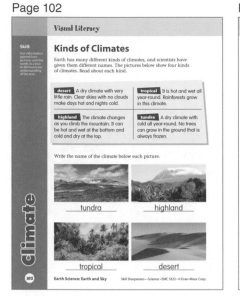

tundra   highland

tropical   desert

Earth Science: Earth and Sky   Skill Sharpeners—Science • EMC 5323 • © Evan-Moor Corp.

climate

102

Page 103

Climate Crossword Puzzle

Use the vocabulary words to complete the crossword puzzle.

greenhouse   tropical   desert   bleach
carbon dioxide   ecosystem   coral reef   climate

Across
2. weather over a long period of time
3. a warm climate where it rains almost every day
4. a gas found in the atmosphere
6. a glass building warmed by the sun

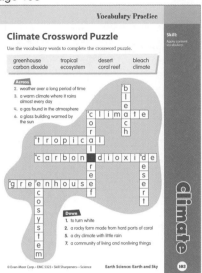

Down
1. to turn white
2. a rocky form made from hard parts of coral
5. a dry climate with little rain
7. a community of living and nonliving things

© Evan-Moor Corp. • EMC 5323 • Skill Sharpeners—Science   Earth Science: Earth and Sky

climate

103

Page 104

Comparing Climates

Skills: Conduct research on a science topic. Complete a table with climate and weather information.

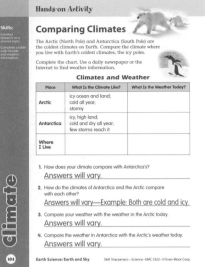

The Arctic (North Pole) and Antarctica (South Pole) are the coldest climates on Earth. Compare the climate where you live with Earth's coldest climates, the icy poles.

Complete the chart. Use a daily newspaper or the Internet to find weather information.

Climates and Weather

Place	What Is the Climate Like?	What Is the Weather Today?
Arctic	icy ocean and land; cold all year; stormy	
Antarctica	icy, high land; cold and dry all year; few storms reach it	
Where I Live		

1. How does your climate compare with Antarctica's?
   Answers will vary.

2. How do the climates of Antarctica and the Arctic compare with each other?
   Answers will vary—Example: Both are cold and icy.

3. Compare your weather with the weather in the Arctic today.
   Answers will vary.

4. Compare the weather in Antarctica with the Arctic's weather today.
   Answers will vary.

Earth Science: Earth and Sky   Skill Sharpeners—Science • EMC 5323 • © Evan-Moor Corp.

climate

104

Page 107

What Is a Hurricane?

Define It!
hurricane: a powerful storm with strong winds and heavy rain
storm surge: rising of the sea
swirl: to spin or whirl
tropical: areas of the Earth that are warm and close to the equator

Concepts: A hurricane is a natural hazard that results from natural processes. Hurricanes have powerful winds. Floods often accompany a hurricane.

Hurricanes are the largest storms on Earth, and they cause the most damage. Hurricanes form in **tropical** areas over warm ocean waters. Often, hurricanes form over the Atlantic Ocean and travel from the west coast of Africa to the east coast of the United States. The storm grows larger as thunderstorm clouds gather in a circle pattern. Storm winds **swirl** around a center. The center of the storm is called the eye of the hurricane.

When hurricanes pass over land, their powerful winds can destroy buildings and tear up trees. A hurricane has winds measuring 74 miles (119 km) per hour and higher. A **storm surge**, or rise of ocean water carried by the hurricane, causes flooding.

Complete the sentences.

1. Hurricanes form in tropical areas because they need
   warm ocean waters

2. Hurricane winds destroy buildings, and a storm surge causes
   flooding

© Evan-Moor Corp. • EMC 5323 • Skill Sharpeners—Science   Earth Science: Earth and Sky

Hurricanes

107

Page 108

Concepts: A hurricane is a natural hazard that humans cannot eliminate, but people can take steps to reduce a hurricane's impact. Meteorologists are weather people who are in the path of a hurricane.

Hurricane Hunters

Define It!
announce: to make known
meteorologist: a weather expert
radar: a tool that uses radio waves to measure the speed of something
satellite: an object sent into space on a rocket to orbit the Earth

Hurricanes can be more than 100 miles (161 km) across and they can travel a long distance. **Meteorologists** (weather scientists) track hurricanes in order to warn people who are in a hurricane's path. Meteorologists use tools such as **radar** and **satellite** pictures from space to see where the hurricane is and in what direction it is going. Special airplanes called *hurricane hunters* gather weather data. These planes sometimes even fly into the eye of a hurricane. The National Weather Service **announces** a *hurricane watch* if there is a good chance of a hurricane forming within 48 hours. A *hurricane warning* means a hurricane is on its way within the next 36 hours, and people should leave that area or find a safe place.

Circle *true* or *false*.

1. Hurricane hunters can stop hurricanes.   true   **false**
2. Satellites help scientists see the path of a hurricane.   **true**   false

Earth Science: Earth and Sky   Skill Sharpeners—Science • EMC 5323 • © Evan-Moor Corp.

Hurricanes

108

Page 109

Hurricane Plans

Define It!
damage: harm that causes loss or makes something worth less
engineer: a person who uses science to plan buildings and other things
property: something that is owned
shutter: a cover for a window that opens and closes on hinges

Concepts: A hurricane is a natural hazard that humans cannot eliminate, but people can take steps to reduce a hurricane's impact. Engineers study hurricane damage in order to create stronger, stronger buildings.

People cannot stop hurricanes, but they can plan ahead to help save lives and **property**. Hurricane Andrew struck the United States in August 1992. It was one of the worst storms in U.S. history. The winds were stronger than 160 miles (257 km) per hour. Andrew destroyed almost the entire city of Homestead, Florida.

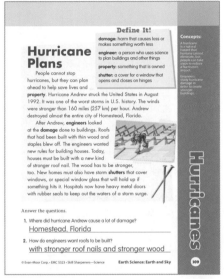

After Andrew, **engineers** looked at the **damage** done to buildings. Roofs that had been built with thin wood and staples blew off. The engineers wanted new rules for building houses. Today, houses must be built with a new kind of stronger roof nail. The wood has to be stronger, too. New homes now also have storm **shutters** that cover windows, or special window glass that will hold up if something hits it. Hospitals now have heavy metal doors with rubber seals to keep out the waters of a storm surge.

Answer the questions.

1. Where did hurricane Andrew cause a lot of damage?
   Homestead, Florida

2. How do engineers want roofs to be built?
   with stronger roof nails and stronger wood

© Evan-Moor Corp. • EMC 5323 • Skill Sharpeners—Science   Earth Science: Earth and Sky

Hurricanes

109

Page 110

A Look from Space

Skills: Label a graphic image to show the working parts of something in nature. Analyze and interpret information presented in both a text and a photo.

The first weather satellite was launched into space in 1960. Today's satellites give meteorologists a good look at hurricanes from space. Satellite pictures taken over time show how fast a hurricane is growing and the path it is taking.

Read the hurricane words and information below. Then label the satellite picture.

Eye The eye is the center of the storm. The eye has calm winds and clear skies. It can be 20 to 40 miles (32 to 64 km) across.

Eye Wall The eye wall is a thick wall of thunderclouds around the eye. The eye wall has the strongest winds and the most rain.

Rain Bands These thick bands of thunderclouds spin around the eye in a pinwheel shape.

Counterclockwise Direction Thunderclouds spin in the opposite direction of the hands of a clock.

Looking at a Hurricane

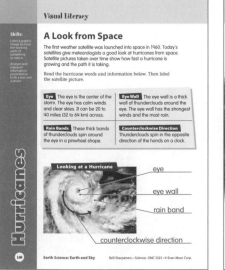

eye
eye wall
rain band
counterclockwise direction

Earth Science: Earth and Sky   Skill Sharpeners—Science • EMC 5323 • © Evan-Moor Corp.

Hurricanes

110

Page 111

Hurricanes Crossword Puzzle

Use the vocabulary words to complete the crossword puzzle.

hurricane   announce   satellite   tropical
meteorologist   engineer   property   radar

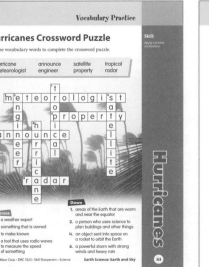

Across
2. a weather expert
5. something that is owned
7. to make known
8. a tool that uses radar to measure the speed of something

Down
1. areas of the Earth that are warm and near the equator
3. a person who uses science to plan buildings and other things
4. an object sent into space on a rocket to orbit the Earth
6. a powerful storm with strong winds and heavy rain

© Evan-Moor Corp. • EMC 5323 • Skill Sharpeners—Science   Earth Science: Earth and Sky

Hurricanes

111

Page 115

Tornado!

Define It!
column: a tall, straight post
occur: to happen
swirl: to spin or whirl
vortex: a mass of whirling air

Concepts: A tornado is a natural hazard that results from natural processes. Tornadoes have powerful, swirling winds.

Tornadoes are some of the strongest storms on Earth. A tornado is a fast-spinning **column** of air, called a **vortex**. It stretches from a thundercloud to the ground. Tornado winds can sometimes spin at 300 miles (483 km) per hour. We are able to see tornado winds because they contain water, dust, and pieces of objects they have picked up. A tornado is powerful enough to lift cars and even houses. The **swirling** winds of a tornado can smash everything in its path. Tornadoes happen in many parts of the world, but most of them **occur** in the United States. About 1,200 tornadoes are reported in the U.S. each year.

Circle *true* or *false*.

1. Tornadoes occur only in the United States.   true   **false**
2. A tornado is a vortex.   **true**   false
3. A tornado is one of Earth's most powerful storms.   **true**   false

© Evan-Moor Corp. • EMC 5323 • Skill Sharpeners—Science   Earth Science: Earth and Sky

Tornadoes

115

Page 116

Tornado Forecast

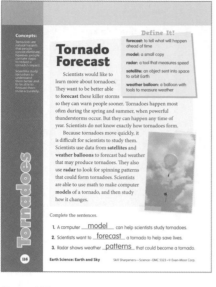

Define It!
- **forecast:** to tell what will happen ahead of time
- **model:** a small copy
- **radar:** a tool that measures speed
- **satellite:** an object sent into space to orbit Earth
- **weather balloon:** a balloon with tools to measure weather

Scientists would like to learn more about tornadoes. They want to be better able to **forecast** these killer storms so they can warn people sooner. Tornadoes happen most often during the spring and summer, when powerful thunderstorms occur. But they can happen any time of year. Scientists do not know exactly how tornadoes form.

Because tornadoes move quickly, it is difficult for scientists to study them. Scientists use data from **satellites** and **weather balloons** to forecast bad weather that may produce tornadoes. They also use **radar** to look for spinning patterns that could form tornadoes. Scientists are able to use math to make computer **models** of a tornado, and then study how it changes.

Complete the sentences.

1. A computer __model__ can help scientists study tornadoes.
2. Scientists want to __forecast__ a tornado to help save lives.
3. Radar shows weather __patterns__ that could become a tornado.

Page 117

Tornado Safety

Define It!
- **drill:** to learn by doing something again and again
- **siren:** an object that makes a loud warning sound
- **storm shelter:** an underground room made to protect people in a tornado

When tornado weather patterns are spotted, the National Weather Service announces a *tornado watch*. This means that people in the area should pay close attention to the sky. They should watch or listen to the TV, the Internet, or a radio for warnings. If a *tornado warning* is given, a tornado has been seen on radar or spotted by someone. It means that people should quickly take cover in a safe place. Some communities sound special **sirens** as a warning.

People need to know ahead of time what to do if a tornado is coming. Tornado **drills** give them practice in where to go and what to do. The safest place to be is underground in a basement or a **storm shelter**. If one of these is not nearby, then go to a small inside room or hallway without windows. People who are outside or in a car should look for a ditch and lie down in it.

Answer the questions.

1. When is a tornado warning given? __when a tornado is seen on radar or someone sees a tornado__
2. Why are tornado drills important? __so people know what to do when a tornado is coming__

Page 118

Visual Literacy

Tornado Count

Since 1950, scientists have kept records of the number of tornadoes in the United States. The total count for 2011 was 1,691. The table below shows how many tornadoes occurred in each month of 2011. Look at the table and answer the questions.

Number of Tornadoes in 2011	
January	16
February	63
March	75
April	758
May	326
June	160
July	103
August	57
September	51
October	23
November	44
December	15

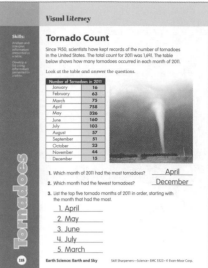

1. Which month of 2011 had the most tornadoes? __April__
2. Which month had the fewest tornadoes? __December__
3. List the top five tornado months of 2011 in order, starting with the month that had the most.
   1. April
   2. May
   3. June
   4. July
   5. March

Page 119

Vocabulary Practice

Either/Or Questions

Write each answer.

1. Is a column like a balloon **or** a post? __post__
2. Is a siren a wind **or** a warning? __warning__
3. In a drill, do you spin **or** practice? __practice__
4. Is a weather balloon used to forecast **or** to play? __forecast__
5. Can radar spot a storm shelter **or** a tornado? __tornado__
6. Is a storm shelter a safe place **or** a model? __safe place__
7. Is a satellite in space **or** underground? __in space__
8. Does a vortex forecast **or** swirl? __swirl__

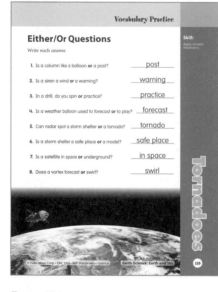

Page 120

Hands-on Activity

Tornado in a Bottle

A tornado is a vortex of swirling winds that forms when a storm causes air to rise very quickly. You can create a model of a swirling vortex with water and two plastic bottles.

What You Need
- 2 clear plastic bottles, empty
- waterproof tape, such as duct tape
- water

What You Do

1. Make sure the bottles are clean, and peel off any labels.
2. Fill one of the bottles two-thirds full with water.
3. Cover the mouth of the empty bottle with tape. Ask an adult to help poke a hole in it. Holes of different sizes will create "tornadoes" with different features.
4. Use tape to fasten the bottles together at the mouth, with the empty one on top. Use enough tape so that no water will leak out. Turn the bottles over so that the water is on top. Immediately swirl the bottles. Look for the vortex inside the top bottle.

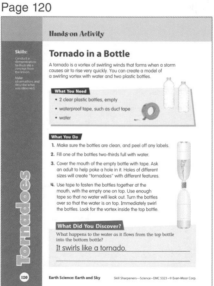

What Did You Discover?
What happens to the water as it flows from the top bottle into the bottom bottle?
__It swirls like a tornado.__

Page 123

Reading

About Floods

Define It!
- **banks:** land at the edge of a river
- **cycle:** a pattern of events that happen in the same order
- **natural hazard:** an event in nature that causes harm to people and property
- **property:** something that is owned

When a body of water covers an area that is usually dry land, that is a flood. Areas near rivers, lakes, and oceans can flood. River floods are the most common. Many rivers have a **cycle** of dry times and flooding. Rivers and lakes may flow over their **banks** when there is more rain than usual, or when snow and ice melt suddenly. Hurricanes can bring floods to areas along ocean coasts.

Although it can sometimes do good things, such as bring new soil to an area, a flood is a **natural hazard**. Farms and crops may be destroyed by a flood. In an area where many people live, floods can be a danger to people's lives. More lives are lost in floods than in any other kind of weather. Floods destroy **property**, and building over again after a flood can cost billions of dollars.

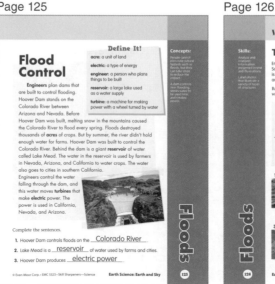

Answer the questions.

1. What can happen to rivers when snow and ice suddenly melt?
   __Rivers can flood.__
2. What can happen to crops in a flood?
   __They can be destroyed.__

Page 124

Ancient Floods

Define It!
- **ancient:** belonging to times long past
- **control:** to hold back
- **dam:** a barrier to hold back water
- **nutrients:** elements in soil that are needed by plants
- **silt:** fine sand or clay carried by water

The Nile River in Africa is the longest river in the world. In **ancient** times in Egypt, the Nile River flooded every year. To the people of ancient Egypt, the flooding Nile was a force of good. The river carried **silt**, or rich new soil. When the floodwaters went away, the rich soil remained. The new soil contained **nutrients** that were good for growing crops. The Nile was so important to the ancient people that their calendar was based on its cycle. The new year began in the middle of summer, when the river began to rise. Today, there is a huge **dam** on the Nile at Aswan, Egypt. The dam was completed in 1970. It **controls** floods in the rainy season and stores water to be used later.

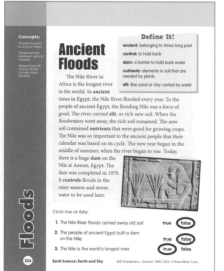

Circle *true* or *false*.

1. The Nile River floods carried away old soil. true **false**
2. The people of ancient Egypt built a dam on the Nile. true **false**
3. The Nile is the world's longest river. **true** false

Page 125

Flood Control

Define It!
- **acre:** a unit of land
- **electric:** a type of energy
- **engineer:** a person who plans things to be built
- **reservoir:** a large lake used as a water supply
- **turbine:** a machine for making power with a wheel turned by water

Engineers plan dams that are built to control flooding. Hoover Dam stands on the Colorado River between Arizona and Nevada. Before Hoover Dam was built, melting snow in the mountains caused the Colorado River to flood every spring. Floods destroyed thousands of **acres** of crops. But by summer, the river didn't hold enough water for farms. Hoover Dam was built to control the Colorado River. Behind the dam is a giant **reservoir** of water called Lake Mead. The water in the reservoir is used by farmers in Nevada, Arizona, and California to water crops. The water also goes to cities in southern California.

Engineers control the water falling through the dam, and this water moves **turbines** that make **electric** power. The power is used in California, Nevada, and Arizona.

Complete the sentences.

1. Hoover Dam controls floods on the __Colorado River__.
2. Lake Mead is a __reservoir__ of water used by farms and cities.
3. Hoover Dam produces __electric power__.

Page 126

Visual Literacy

Types of Dams

Engineers build dams in different shapes and with different materials. Some dams are made from earth and others from concrete. Concrete is sand, stones, cement, and water mixed together. Concrete hardens and becomes very strong.

Read about each type of dam. Then label the pictures to tell which type of dam each one is.

Embankment Dam An embankment is a wall or bank of earth. The Fort Peck Dam in Montana is an embankment dam.

Gravity Dam It is thick and made of concrete. Its huge weight holds back the water. The Grand Coulee Dam in Washington state is a gravity dam.

Buttress Dam Tall supports called *buttresses* hold up the dam. The Bartlett Dam in Arizona is a buttress dam.

Arch Dam It has a curved shape and is often built between two walls of rock. The Glen Canyon Dam in Arizona is an arch dam.

1. Glen Canyon Dam — __arch dam__
2. Bartlett Dam — __buttress dam__
3. Grand Coulee Dam — __gravity dam__
4. Fort Peck Dam — __embankment dam__

Page 127

Vocabulary Practice

Floods Crossword Puzzle

Use the vocabulary words to complete the crossword puzzle.

Skill: Apply content vocabulary.

banks   engineer   cycle   dam
ancient   reservoir   silt   turbine

Crossword answers:
- turbine
- cycle
- silt
- reservoir
- engineer
- banks
- ancient
- dam

Across
3. a machine for making power with a wheel turned by water
4. fine sand or clay carried by water
5. a person who plans things to be built
8. belonging to times long past

Down
1. a pattern of events that happen in the same order
2. a large lake used as a water supply
6. land at the edge of a river
7. a barrier to hold back water

© Evan-Moor Corp. • EMC 5323 • Skill Sharpeners—Science   **Earth Science: Earth and Sky**   127

Page 129

Make a Working Waterwheel, continued

4. Cut ½" (1.3 cm) slits into the edge of the first paper plate, about 2" (5 cm) apart. Fit a flap into each slit on the paper plate, slits together as shown.

5. Tie the paper clip to one end of the yarn. Decide where on the pencil to tie the other end of the yarn. Then test your idea.

6. Lay the ends of the pencil on your open hands with palms up, so both the waterwheel and the pencil can turn. Let the yarn and the paper clip drop down from the pencil. Hold the waterwheel over the sink in a stream of water as shown.

7. The wheel will turn, causing the pencil to spin. The yarn should wind around the pencil, lifting the paper clip.

What Did You Discover?

Did your idea work?
Answers will vary.

What happens when you slide the yarn to a different place on the pencil? Explain.
Answers will vary.

Can you make the yarn unwind and lower the paper clip? How?
Yes, by holding the waterwheel so it turns in the opposite direction.

© Evan-Moor Corp. • EMC 5323 • Skill Sharpeners—Science   **Earth Science: Earth and Sky**   129

Page 130

Application

Skill: Write informative text to examine different views of the impact of a natural hazard.

Thinking About Floods

There is more than one way to think about floods. Floods are a natural hazard, but the people of ancient Egypt considered them to be a good thing.

Write some ideas to support each way of thinking.

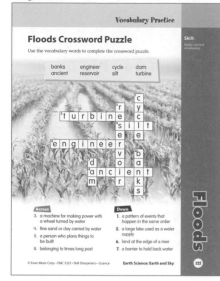
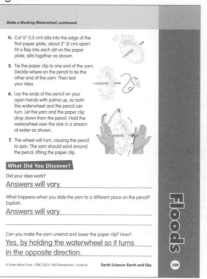

1. Floods are a natural hazard.
   Answers will vary—Example: Floods destroy crops and property. Lives may be lost. It costs billions of dollars to build again.

2. In ancient Egypt, floods were helpful.
   Answers will vary—Example: The flooding Nile brought silt that was rich in nutrients. The new soil was good for growing crops.

130   **Earth Science: Earth and Sky**   Skill Sharpeners—Science • EMC 5323 • © Evan-Moor Corp.

Here's how parents turn "I'm bored! There's nothing to do!" into "I'm *never* bored!"

The Never-Bored Kid Books

Ages 4–9 This exciting, colorful series will engage kids in hours of productive fun. There are hidden pictures, puzzles, things to cut out and create, pop-ups, art projects, word games, and a whole lot more! **evan-moor.com/nbkb**

The Never-Bored Kid Book

Ages 4–5	EMC 6300
Ages 5–6	EMC 6303
Ages 6–7	EMC 6301
Ages 7–8	EMC 6304
Ages 8–9	EMC 6302

160 full-color pages.

The Never-Bored Kid Book 2

Ages 4–5	EMC 6307
Ages 5–6	EMC 6308
Ages 6–7	EMC 6309
Ages 7–8	EMC 6310
Ages 8–9	EMC 6311

144 full-color pages.

*iParenting Media Hot Award Winner

Flashcards

These aren't your average flashcards! Our flashcards include an interactive component with access to online timed tests. The corresponding online activities add another dimension to flashcard practice. Each flashcard set motivates young learners to practice an important readiness concept or fundamental skill.

56 full-color flashcards

56 full-color flashcards.
AGES 4–7+

Reading

Colors and Shapes	Ages 4+	EMC 4161
The Alphabet	Ages 4+	EMC 4162
Vowel Sounds	Ages 5+	EMC 4163
Word Families	Ages 6+	EMC 4164
Sight Words	Ages 6+	EMC 4165

Math

Counting 1–20	Ages 4+	EMC 4166
Counting 1–100	Ages 5+	EMC 4167
Addition and Subtraction Facts to 10	Ages 5+	EMC 4168
Addition Facts 11–18	Ages 6+	EMC 4169
Subtraction Facts 11–18	Ages 6+	EMC 4170
Multiplication Facts to 9s	Ages 7+	EMC 4171
Division Facts to 9s	Ages 7+	EMC 4172

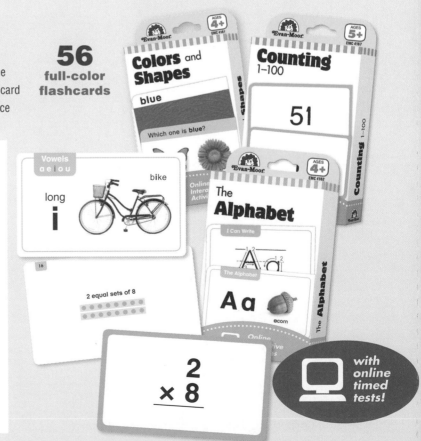

with online timed tests!

Daily Science

Spark students' imaginations with thought-provoking questions and build science vocabulary and comprehension!

Based on Science Standards for Life, Earth, and Physical Sciences.

Grades 1–6 *Why do camels have humps? How far up does the sky reach? Where do echoes come from?* These are just some of the motivating questions your students will answer while they investigate the standards-based scientific concepts in *Daily Science*. Thirty weeks of 10- to 15-minute lessons introduce students to physical-, life-, and earth-science concepts while they find the answers to real-life questions about the world around them. 192 reproducible pages. Correlated to U.S. standards.

Daily Science

Teacher's Edition

Grade 1	EMC 5011	ISBN 978-1-59673-419-7
Grade 2	EMC 5012	ISBN 978-1-59673-420-3
Grade 3	EMC 5013	ISBN 978-1-59673-421-0
Grade 4	EMC 5014	ISBN 978-1-59673-928-4
Grade 5	EMC 5015	ISBN 978-1-59673-929-1
Grade 6	EMC 5016	ISBN 978-1-59673-930-7

Student Book 5-Pack

Grade 1	EMC 6621	ISBN 978-1-59673-422-7
Grade 2	EMC 6622	ISBN 978 1 59673 423 4
Grade 3	EMC 6623	ISBN 978-1-59673-424-1
Grade 4	EMC 6624	ISBN 978-1-59673-931-4
Grade 5	EMC 6625	ISBN 978-1-59673-932-1
Grade 6	EMC 6626	ISBN 978-1-59673-933-8

Interactive Also Available

Grade 3

Class Packs
Set of 20 Student Books + Teacher's Edition

Daily Science

Class Pack
Set of 20 Student Books + Teacher's Edition

Grade 1	EMC 9655	ISBN 978-1-60823-594-0
Grade 2	EMC 9656	ISBN 978-1-60823-595-7
Grade 3	EMC 9657	ISBN 978-1-60823-596-4
Grade 4	EMC 9658	ISBN 978-1-60823-597-1
Grade 5	EMC 9659	ISBN 978-1-60823-598-8
Grade 6	EMC 9660	ISBN 978-1-60823-599-5

At-Home Tutor

A one-of-a-kind collection of educational activities with access to online timed tests!

Truly the Best!

Curriculum-based reading and math skills are presented in fun, engaging activities to inspire genuine learning.

Perfect for...

- extra practice
- constructive free time
- review during school breaks
- getting ready for the next level
- vacations and car trips